AI In Healthcare

A Science-backed Guide to Stay Ahead in Your Career,
Bridge the Gap Between Technology and Patient Care,
Safeguard Your Position and Enhance Your Expertise
With Cutting-edge Insights

V. Soltis

Contents

Book Description

Master patient care with AI-driven innovations in just a few months, even if AI seems overwhelming right now!

Are you struggling to keep up with the rapid pace of AI technology in healthcare?

Are you concerned about effectively integrating AI without losing the personal touch in patient care?

How do I align AI tools with strict regulations and ethical standards?

You're not alone. Many healthcare professionals and tech enthusiasts face these challenges. Yet, with the right insights and strategies, the hurdles can be overcome.

AI in Healthcare – Virtual Health Assistants bridge the gap between cutting-edge AI innovations and accessible healthcare, unlocking the transformative potential of virtual health assistants to guide patients through long-distance treatments and aftercare.

Here's just a taste of what you'll discover inside this forward-thinking guide:

- **The 7-step framework for seamlessly integrating AI in clinical settings**
- **Real-world case studies showcasing successful AI implementation in patient care**
- **Five crucial steps to balance AI efficiency with the warmth of human interactions**
- **The impact of AI chatbots on streamlining aftercare processes**
- **How to navigate complex regulations and comply with privacy laws**
- **Insights into predictive analytics driving better treatment outcomes**
- **Integrating AI without compromising on ethical considerations**
- **How leading institutions are using AI to enhance patient satisfaction and experience**
- **Top 5 myths debunked about AI replacing Healthcare jobs**
- **The future trends of AI in healthcare you need to be prepared for**
- **Investment risks and opportunities in the AI healthcare sector**
- **How AI chatbots are redefining mental health support and outreach**
- **Techniques to reassure patients and build trust in AI-driven solutions**
- **Solutions for identifying and addressing AI algorithm biases**
- **Key considerations when selecting an AI vendor for your facility**

...and so much more!

We understand the skepticism around AI: the fear that it will over-shadow human empathy, the intimidation by its technical intricacies, and the worry that it will be just a fleeting trend.

But the truth is that AI in healthcare is here to stay, facilitating improvements that enhance rather than replace the human touch.

This guide is not another theoretical textbook; it's crafted to empower anyone looking to harness AI's potential in healthcare settings. With relatable language and practical examples, even non-tech profes-sionals can use this knowledge.

Introduction

A few years ago, while I was running an agency for elderly care, an event altered my healthcare perspective forever. I had a client who was finding it hard to keep up with their complicated medication routine. and needed extra help that was beyond what my team could physically offer. This situation gave me a vivid understanding of the restrictions in ordinary care methods. One evening, I chanced upon an article discussing AI-driven health helpers. The thought that tech could fill in patient care gaps inspired my interest. I saw that AI can change how we care for, and support patients, even remotely. This book's content delves into AI's unbelievable capacity to remodel healthcare. AI can enhance patient support, help make diagnoses better, and smoothen the processes. These are not merely ideas for the future, but current realities. I aim to offer healthcare workers, and creative thinkers, helpful knowledge of how AI can revolutionize their profession. Whether you are a doctor, a nurse, or a tech fan, this book presents a guide for merging AI into your work routine. Its content is wide-ranging, but targeted. We'll consider AI's part in diagnoses, planning treatments, patient care, and ethical issues—important areas in modern healthcare innovation. The intention is to make AI comprehensible for everyone, regardless of their technical knowledge level. I want to break down AI to let you see that it's a device for improving healthcare, not replacing human workers. The readers we're targeting are doctors, nurses, medical technicians, health tech fans, investors, and policymakers, who all have an interest in the future of healthcare. This book matters because AI is currently transforming your field. Grasping these changes is vital for career development, and adjustment to new issues. In the book, we'll delve into crucial topics such as bridging the gap between tech and healthcare, the practical effects of AI, and managing legal and ethical ramifications. These topics are closely linked. They prove how AI can improve our work without removing the crucial human touch specific to healthcare.

This book is a journey. Imagine it as a step-by-step guide starting at the beginning, growing your knowledge with every page. Right now, learning about AI in healthcare is really important, and by the time you finish, you'll see the whole picture. The tech world is changing fast, and so is healthcare. It's not just good to know about it, it's also important to understand it. This book provides handy information, and plans you can use. It shares real life examples, thoughts from experts, and step-by-step plans for using AI in your work. Everything you need to feel secure, and confident, in this new world is provided. As we finish this intro, I encourage you to see AI as a chance for exciting changes, and better patient care. It's not about following the latest thing, but helping shape healthcare's future. Together, we can ensure tech works for us, making healthcare faster, more personal, and easier for everyone.

1. Foundations of AI in Healthcare

1.1 Demystifying AI: Breaking Down Complex Concepts

In simple terms, Artificial intelligence (AI) is all about teaching computers to act like humans. It's about getting machines to learn, think, and correct themselves, like humans do. One of the central parts of AI is termed the "Artificial Neural Network" (ANN). This bit is made to mirror the network of neurons in our brain. Thanks to this, computers can recognize patterns, and make decisions on their own. Take a scenario where you use AI to study a large amount of data, like hospital records. The AI can spot patterns that we can't, and can shape how we treat patients. AI plays a significant role in healthcare; thanks to something we call "Natural Language Processing" (NLP). NLP lets machines understand, and react to human talk. AI chatbots, for instance, use NLP to talk to patients, gather their health histories, and spot health patterns. This helps doctors diagnose more accurately, and keeps patients engaged, by offering round-the-clock support. Imagine a situation where a patient tells their symptoms to a virtual assistant. The assistant then gives initial advice, or arranges for the patient to meet a doctor. The interaction is seamless, thanks to NLP, and has changed how we get, and provide, healthcare.

Next, I want to introduce you to "computer vision", another intriguing part of AI. It allows machines to understand visual data from our world, and in healthcare, it helps to scrutinize medical images, like X-rays and MRIs, more accurately than humans. Computer vision assists radiologists in spotting irregularities early, which could save lives, by starting treatment sooner. To navigate the world of AI in healthcare, it's essential to understand some standard terms. Algorithms, which are sets of rules, or steps, taken to solve problems, form the backbone of AI. They enable machines to do specific tasks, from forecasting how a patient will do, to suggesting treatment plans. We often speak about "machine learning", and "deep learning". Machine learning involves getting computers to learn from data, to improve over time, without specific programming. Deep learning, which is a subset of machine learning, uses several layers of neural networks to examine large amounts of data. This makes it especially useful for tricky tasks, like image and voice recognition. Finally, automation in healthcare means using AI to do regular tasks. This lets healthcare professionals focus more on caring for the patient, and less on paperwork.

AI technology is quickly progressing. In the last few years, it has grown exponentially because of more access to data, and better computer power. One of the primary uses of AI is in the healthcare world. It makes a big difference in finding diseases early and, creating customized patient treatments, (Source 2). AI has improved healthcare, given us new ways to study, and invent new treatments. All this is leading us to a time when AI might be vital in staying healthy, but people need to understand what AI does. Some people are afraid that AI will take the place of doctors, and nurses, but AI is actually a tool to help them do their jobs better, not replace them. For example, AI can help by analyzing medical pictures quickly, but doctors still diagnose the issues, and develop the treatment plans. People also think that AI works on its own, without any control, but that's not true. It works best when it works with people in a hospital, doctor's office, or clinic setting. Together, people and AI can deliver the best health outcomes for patients. By understanding these misconceptions about AI, we can have more valuable talks about how it can help healthcare professionals, while addressing any worries about using it.

1.2 Workings of Machine Learning in Healthcare

Machine learning is an integral part of AI for healthcare. It allows computers to study data, understand it, and make decisions. This means doctors can predict how a patient's health might change, and assess risks in a better way. As an example, machine learning can use a patient's past health data to guess possible future health issues. This allows doctors to take early action, and is very helpful in managing long-term diseases, or predicting complications, which ultimately improves patient care, and lowers costs. By identifying patterns in the data, machine learning supports doctors in making informed decisions quickly, which is reasonably necessary in fast-paced situations like in an emergency room.

Machine learning helps to solve different problems. In one popular model, supervised learning, machines get trained on datasets where the solutions are already known. It's somewhat like teaching a student with examples, and answers, enabling the machine to understand the relationship between inputs and outputs. It can learn to guess if a person would get sick by looking at past health data. Unsupervised learning is a bit different; it's about finding hidden trends or structures in the data, without prior knowledge or examples – imagine exploring a place with no map. This model helps categorize patients into groups for targeted healthcare. A third model, called reinforcement learning, involves teaching machines, by rewarding and punishing, good and bad actions. It shows promise in making healthcare plans, where the machine learns the best ways to get better patient results by trying, and improving gradually. Machine learning is already making a big splash in healthcare. One great example is the way it's used in spotting things in medical images faster, and more accurately, than humans. This makes diagnoses more correct, and speeds up the process, freeing up time for doctors to focus on more challenging cases...and that's not all. Machine learning turns spoken, or written, medical notes into organized data, making record-keeping easier, and reducing the workload for health professionals, which means doctors can spend more time with their patients, not on paperwork. Despite all these benefits, using machine learning in healthcare does come with challenges. Data privacy is a big issue. Safeguarding patient data against unauthorized access, and leaks, is critical. In addition, the quality and availability of data are crucial, too; insufficient data can cause wrong models, and faulty guesses. As machine learning influences crucial medical decisions, it's key to understand and lessen bias in these models. Bias could arise if the data used to train machines doesn't represent the diverse patients the healthcare system serves, leading to biased results that could affect patient care. So, continuous watch, and improvement of these models, are needed to ensure they're accurate and fair.

Simply put, machine learning is a powerful tool for healthcare. It improves the way we analyze data, and guess future outcomes. This means doctors can better decide the types of care their patients might need. Of course, there are some hurdles, like privacy and ethics, but if we address them properly, machine learning can improve healthcare.

1.3. Deep Learning in Diagnostics: Why It's a Big Deal

Deep learning is a massive leap forward in artificial intelligence, especially in healthcare testing. This smart tech works like the human brain, using math tricks layered together, to examine a lot of information. For example, Convolutional Neural Networks (CNNs) are important in this field, as they specialize in looking at images. CNNs can spot patterns and details in medical pictures, therefore, they're superb at finding issues in X-rays, or MRI scans, that human eyes might miss. They can spot early tumor signs by noticing minor changes in body tissue, so catching these details early can save lives. Recurrent Neural Networks (RNNs), are another type of deep learning. They're used to process data that come one after another, making them useful in healthcare. They can, for instance, analyze data collected over time from patient check-up systems. RNNs can predict future health issues by studying old patterns, akin to how a doctor might guess a patient's recovery process based on old health records. They are good at understanding how a patient's health changes over time. This can be vital in managing long-lasting diseases, or creating long-term care plans. Deep learning is making a strange, but positive, difference in healthcare testing. A good example is early detection of diabetic blindness. Algorithms made with deep learning study pictures of the eye, spotting disease signs with incredible accuracy. This lets doctors step in, and start treatment sooner, which can improve the patient's health. In another example, deep learning has automated the detection of tumors in MRI scans. By teaching these learning models with many images, scientists have created math tricks that recognize tumor locations, and guess how they will grow. This boosts the accuracy of diagnoses, and aids doctors in planning better treatments.

More and more, doctors and hospitals are using smart tools to help get better at their jobs. There are platforms called TensorFlow, and PyTorch, that are helping with medical research. These tools help doctors develop ways to find, and solve, problems. They are also easy to change, and grow, allowing doctors to create solutions for different diagnoses. Extra-special hardware, like GPUs, helps these tools work better, by making complex tasks simple to complete. It also helps to speed up training, and lets big piles of data be studied quickly and correctly. In the future, these smart tools might change how we spot health problems. One idea being investigated is real-time diagnoses. Imagine if a gadget you wear could keep checking your health, while a smart tool sifts through the data to find anything odd. This could help stop serious problems, before they even start, shifting the focus from treatment, to stopping illnesses in their tracks. We might also see these smart tools mixing with other new technologies. Mixing smart tools with genetic data could make personalized medicine possible, leading to tailor-made treatments for your genes. This could let doctors predict how well medication will work for a patient, avoiding side effects, and improving treatments. These smart tools have already shown how they can help spot illnesses faster, and more accurately. We'll likely see them put to new uses as they improve, giving us fresh methods for better patient care. There's no doubt that these tools will lead to new discoveries that will completely change healthcare. By embracing these tools, doctors can provide better diagnoses, and superior patient outcomes.

1.4 Big Data's Role in AI-Driven Healthcare

Healthcare's Big Data isn't just a fancy term, it's key to breakthroughs in modern medicine. Vast amounts of information, from digital health records to genetic details, make up this big data. Digital records contain a patient's medical background, with more information about illnesses, treatments, and outcomes. When used correctly, this chunky wad of data gives precious insights for better patient care. There's also something called genomic data in the mix. Genomic data is like a roadmap of a person's genes, opening the door to tailor-made medicine. This means healthcare providers can make treatments more personal by taking into account a patient's unique genetic code, and health history. Turning this raw data into valuable insights, or "big data analytics", as it's called, is key. Using clever algorithms and analyses, these analytics spot patterns in patient data. This allows for healthcare that's more suitable and effective. As an example, spotting trends in health records can flag potential health concerns ahead of time. This early warning system lets healthcare workers act sooner, preventing serious issues, and sparking better patient results. Additionally, by identifying risk groups, and adjusting interventions to meet their needs, big data analytics help in managing general health. In doing so, resources are put to better use, and public health gets a boost. Still, merging extensive data from different sources isn't easy. One major hurdle is ensuring multiple health IT systems "speak the same language". Often, various systems have their templates and norms, which bucks against smooth data sharing and integration. This results in "data silos", blocking the complete analyses we need for tip-top healthcare. The need for data privacy, and accuracy, is also paramount. The sensitivity of healthcare data means breaches could severely harm patient confidentiality, which is why "data anonymization" is critical. It masks personal identifiers, letting researchers and healthcare providers use the data without threatening privacy.

Thanks to new tech and lots of data, big changes are happening in healthcare. A good example of this is the Johns Hopkins Precision Medicine project. This project uses big data to make treatments that work just for you. It pulls data from electronic health records, gene information, and more, to give you personal care. This can make you healthier, and lower the cost of healthcare. IBM's Watson is also shining in this field, by helping to find new drugs faster. Thanks to its power to process large amounts of data, Watson can review many science articles and test results. It helps to make new treatments faster, raising the chance of finding good medicines for hard-to-treat diseases. As we look ahead, big data can bring many good changes to healthcare. Better ways of joining and analyzing data can open new possibilities for improving healthcare. Improvement in analyzing data quickly and correctly can lead to new breakthroughs in patient care. Big data analysis is becoming even more important in the future. It can make healthcare more efficient, more personal, and better. Healthcare providers can use the insights from big data to make treatments that work better for patients. This could greatly improve the quality of care. It's a big change in healthcare, where decisions are made based on data. This leads to better, faster, and more patient-focused healthcare.

2. Integrating AI into Clinical Practice

I magine being in a busy hospital, with doctors and nurses speeding down halls, and patients waiting to be seen. Every tick of the clock matters in such a place, and everyone has to be precise in their tasks. During a frantic day at my elder care center, I saw for myself how smart tech could change a potential disaster, into well-oiled teamwork. We had just started using an AI program that takes care of patient files, and treatment times; it was a game changer right away. People who once lost hours flipping through files, could spend time with patients instead, and they could tweak the care they gave to fit each person better. Seeing this made me a believer in how AI can improve healthcare work, and that belief runs through everything I write in this part. We'll dig into the tactical moves for effective AI use in healthcare centers, focusing on checking readiness, crafting thorough plans, bringing everyone on board, and testing ideas. Before leaping headfirst into AI use, reading your company's AI-preparedness is key. This means a deep-dive review of where you are in terms of system setup, team abilities, and current tech. Doing a tech check-up is a must at the onset. It shines a light on the good, and bad, bits of your current systems, pointing out spots where AI could fit in nicely. For instance, you might find out that your data storage needs a facelift, meaning upgrades are required to take on the heavy-duty data work of AI. Along with tech checks, sizing up workforce talents is just as vital. Determine if your team has the skills to use AI tools, or needs more training. This can spotlight education gaps that have to be fixed to make the switch to AI workflow painless. Training might cover a wide range of topics, from grasping simple AI ideas, to nailing down exact AI instruments relevant to your services. Having a detailed game plan for AI action is up next, once you know how ready you are. This strategy should list clear, attainable goals, for your group's patient care, and efficiency ambitions. Having achievable objectives ensures that AI brings real benefits, without overloading your staff.

Think about your AI goals, and what they could look like now; making more accurate diagnoses, boosting interactions with patients, and cutting down paperwork, can be very beneficial. Once you've set your goals, use your resources smartly. This means saving money for new tech, training, and ongoing backup. Choosing where to put your resources should be thought out, making sure you have everything, and everyone, you need to get your AI plans up and running. Good resource planning can stop things from backing up, and ensure the AI tools are implemented without a hitch. Getting a wide range of people involved is key to making AI work. Let your medical staff have a say in decisions, get their input, and support. They see how patient care works firsthand, and can share helpful suggestions about how AI can make their jobs easier, and more efficient. Working with the IT folks and vendors makes sure that the AI tools are technically solid, and fit with what your organization needs. The IT pros can check how well the new tech matches what you already have, and vendors can give tips about the best ways to get it going. Building team spirit helps you tackle any pushback, and creates a feeling of ownership among everyone involved. This ensures that the move to AI is welcomed and works well.

Interactive Component: How Prepared Are You for AI?

- Give Your Tech a Check-up: Look at your current tech and see where AI could slip in.
- Skills Test for Your Team: Find out what training the team needs, and implement schemes to fix any skills deficits.
- Goals Set in Stone: Write down precise goals for using AI to care for patients, and manage things.
- Where's The Money? Plan out funding for tech, training, and backup.
- Get Everyone Onboard: Bring the medical staff, IT folks, and those who sell the tech into the plan.

The last move in the game plan to bring in AI, is to test and scale AI answers to problems. Start by pinpointing areas in your organization that are primed and ready for an AI makeover. These test areas should need AI answers, and be happy to try new tech. For instance, an X-ray unit might be perfect for testing AI tools that study images, because they deal with a boatload of diagnostic imagery. As soon as you have picked the test areas, AI will be ushered in under controlled conditions, and data and input will be gathered to see how well it works. Look closely at data to find problem areas, or things needing a polish-up, tweaking things as you go. Doing this lets you fine-tune AI, before unveiling it in other areas of your handiwork. Meticulously testing AI means you get a smooth transition into using it everywhere, reaping all its benefits, and keeping patient care trouble-free.

2.1 Telemedicine and AI: Enhancing Remote Patient Care

Telemedicine, boosted by AI, is changing how we get medical care, especially when in-person visits are not possible. Thanks to upgrades in tech, doctors can help patients, even from a distance. AI is guiding this shift, offering new ways to treat patients outside clinics and hospitals. For example, a new tool run by AI helps patients check possible health issues. A patient inputs their symptoms into a system, the AI gives an early review, and suggests if they need to see a doctor, or not. This tech means less strain on medical centers, with the added bonus that patients get quick health information, in the privacy of their own homes. AI also supports patients via virtual healthcare workers who answer questions, remind patients to take their meds, and are helpful with persistent sickness management. Watching a patient's health, and giving regular support, is very important, but AI-powered telemedicine offers more than just symptom checks. An added benefit is more people can get health services, and is great for those in remote or forgotten areas. Patients can meet with doctors without traveling far, saving time, and is more convenient for some. AI tech also lets doctors monitor patients' health updates in real-time. They get feedback, and can tweak treatment plans if necessary, improving health results. Using a patient's health facts and history, AI can even offer personalized treatment suggestions, meaning each one gets high-quality, and satisfying care. That said, adding AI to telemedicine is not without its issues. Above all, patient data must be treated carefully to respect privacy. AI in telemedicine must stick to strong data protection rules, using safe methods to share data, and codes, for protection. Cross-border laws on telemedicine also make things difficult. As this service spreads worldwide, it has to follow different rules in different countries. Telemedicine providers need to plan, and work hand in hand, with legal experts. In this way, all the services meet the required rules.

AI's effect on online healthcare is shown through real stories. It is super helpful when looking after long-term illnesses from far away. For instance, people with diabetes can use special AI-powered online health systems. They can keep tabs on their blood sugar, get advice on what to eat, and change how much medicine they take. If there is a problem, these systems can tell them immediately. This way, they can do something about it early, and avoid serious health problems. AI also helps a lot with mental health care. Online mental health helpers can guide therapy sessions, track the patient's progress, and offer help immediately in tough times. Thanks to AI, these services are available to more people, making it easier for them to seek help.

2.2 Wearables and Predictive Analytics in Patient Monitoring

Using AI with wearable tech brings new ways to watch over patients. It makes healthcare quicker to respond to, and can be tailored to each person. These AI-powered wearables, think smartwatch, are more than just gadgets that count your daily steps, they can also constantly monitor your health, and vitals. Imagine a device on your wrist that keeps an eye on your heart rhythm, can quickly warn you when something's not right, and immediately summon emergency services. For people with heart conditions, like atrial fibrillation, this can be a lifesaver. Wearable glucose monitors are another great example of AI's power. People with diabetes use these devices to continuously monitor their blood sugar levels, saving them from having to prick their fingers all the time, which can be painful. AI looks at the data from these monitors, finds trends, and can foresee any big changes in glucose levels. This ability to predict changes makes it easier for patients to manage their health better, and gives doctors helpful information to update treatment plans. AI takes patient care to another level with predictive analytics, meaning it predicts health needs, before they become serious problems. Algorithms look at the data from wearables to foresee serious health events, like heart attacks, or strokes. They do this by noting slight changes in vital signs that suggest stress, or weird activity. This enables doctors to act early, and provide care that may prevent major health crises. With long-term issues, like asthma or COPD, predictive analytics keeps an eye out for returning symptoms, and ensures that patients get treatment adjustments on time. Catching these early warning signs means fewer hospital stays, better patient results, which leads to a healthcare system that works better, and is more effective.

These exciting technologies have potential drawbacks, including significant data privacy and safety concerns. Data from AI-powered wearable gadgets can be delicate, as they often share private health information about a person. Protecting this information from unwanted access through secure data transfer methods is important. It is critical to ensure data is safe while it moves between gadgets or healthcare systems, as is getting user consent on data ownership. Individuals must understand how their data is used, and who can access it. Openness, and strong consent processes, are important for building trust, and getting people to use wearables in healthcare. Real-life examples show how these AI-powered wearable devices can impact patient care, and health results. Let's look at detecting a heart condition called atrial fibrillation earlier than usual. Wearables with AI software have been used to find this condition in people without symptoms. These devices helped prevent serious health issues, by letting people know they needed to see a doctor. In the fitness and wellness world, these wearables provide personalized health information, allowing users to set proper bodily goals. Whether finding the best workout routine, or monitoring sleep habits, these insights help people make choices that improve their health, and overall wellness.

2.3 Overcoming Integration Challenges: Real-World Solutions

To be clear, using AI in hospitals isn't a walk in the park. The biggest issue is the way it works together with other systems. Many hospitals use old systems that don't talk well with the new AI tech. This can cause issues with information getting stuck in hard-to-reach places. Another problem is how folks react to change. Professionals in healthcare have their way of doing things, and may worry that a translator that helps different systems talk to, and understand each other, will be complicated. IT helps overcome issues by changing data, so the AI can work better with older systems. Another helpful solution is cloud-based AI tech. This option enables hospitals to use powerful AI tools without changing the physical tech in the building. Cloud solutions give flexibility, and allow quick changes based on needs, or new tech developments, but technical solutions alone won't cut it. The way we think, and work as a team, is just as important. We can manage change smoothly by training people to use AI, and involve them in the process. It's also critical for leaders to show their support. If leaders get behind AI changes, and highlight the benefits, it can build trust in AI and foster new ideas. The backing from top-level folks can help everyone see AI as a helping hand, not a threat. Promoting a learning and innovation-friendly environment can also help in smashing cultural roadblocks. We can learn how hospitals have cleverly tackled these challenges from real-world examples. One way is by creating diverse teams that look at the problems from different angles.

Lots of different experts, from doctors to computer whizzes, work together. They spot problems, find answers, and use AI tools to simplify tasks. Always listening, and improving things, helps make AI work well with what's already happening. By asking staff and patients what they think, teams can improve things. This way, AI keeps changing to match people's needs, and works better for everyone. Working together, and having a game plan for using AI, is super important. AI could do incredible things if hospitals overcome tech issues, and get everyone onboard. As we progress, blending AI into healthcare seamlessly will significantly help in patient care, and make everyday tasks faster. In the next part, we'll talk about how AI changes jobs in healthcare, allowing specialists to work better and more efficiently. This new way of doing things betters patient care, provides fresh chances for learning, and improves the healthcare industry.

3. AI's Impact on Healthcare Roles

In our modern hospitals, a quiet change is happening. One day, while I watched a nurse work, I noticed there was a slight change in what she was doing. She didn't have to do as much paperwork, or data entry, making it possible for her to spend more time with patients, talking to, and listening to them. This change didn't happen because there were more staff, it happened because of new AI technology. It helped with routine tasks, giving her time to focus on what matters – caring for patients. That's the real power of AI in healthcare. It supports, and changes roles, to help people do better. AI is changing healthcare roles in a big way. It helps with routine tasks, which allows healthcare workers to focus on complex, patient-centered work. One good example is AI-powered diagnostic tools. They can take a good look at medical images, find anything unusual, and complete reports, making it possible for radiologists to have a detailed discussion about treatment options with their patients. This shift means better care for patients, and also makes their experience more positive. In much the same way, automating administrative tasks, like scheduling and billing, makes things smoother. Healthcare workers can then focus on giving total care, being present for their patients, and not being glued to a desk. AI does more than automate tasks, it makes better decisions through teamwork. Think about the part AI plays in planning and carrying out operations. Surgeons can now work with AI systems that think about all the data beforehand, and suggest the best way to move forward. This minimizes risks, and improves success rates. It's a perfect example of the benefits of combining human knowledge, and machine accuracy. AI also helps pull together enormous amounts of patient data. This helps health-care teams develop treatment plans that are just right for each patient, making healthcare more tailored to the individual. As AI technology advances, it is causing changes to roles in healthcare. New roles, like AI system managers and data analysts, are being created. We need these kinds of experts more and more, because they manage, and understand, AI technology. AI system managers ensure AI applications work well, and are aligned with the clinic's needs. Data analysts, on the other hand, interpret AI-driven insights. They turn data into plans of action for taking care of patients. These types of roles are vital for bringing AI into healthcare. They help bridge the gap between technology, and practice, making sure we get the most out of AI systems.

In simplified words, many good examples show the positive results of bringing AI into health-related jobs. For example, it has changed diag-noses in areas like scanning departments. AI systems can look at medical images with outstanding accuracy. This helps the radiologists work better, and gives them time to focus on complex cases requiring human judgment. AI technology also lessens mistakes made in diag-noses, and boosts work efficiency. It ensures patients are diagnosed properly, and quickly. In the same way, AI aids nurses in educating patients. AI-powered platforms offer patients tailored information, support, and encourages patients to play an active part in their own health. These examples underline how AI helps healthcare jobs improve patient results, and satisfaction. Reflect on How AI could change your current job, or daily routines. Think about the regular tasks that eat up your time. Can AI help lighten such loads? Picture how this change could improve your interactions with patients, and raise the quality of care you offer. Ponder on teamwork opportunities that AI might open up. This would allow you to use AI-powered insights to make more informed decisions. Consider whether your job could become more specialized, and if you could take on new tasks related to managing AI systems, or analyzing data. Remember the success stories from this chapter, and visualize how such break-throughs could be used in your daily routines. While thinking about this, try to answer these questions: Could AI free up your time for activities centered on patients? What teamwork opportunities could AI bring to your routines? Could you learn new skills or take up new tasks as AI grows in healthcare? By answering these questions, you can better realize the change AI could bring to healthcare, and then imagine how it could improve your job journey.

3.1 Embracing AI: Training Programs for Professional Growth

As AI increasingly becomes a part of the healthcare landscape, the need to identify training requirements for healthcare professionals grows more urgent. Understanding AI algorithms, and their applications, is crucial. It's about more than just knowing what AI can do, but comprehending how these algorithms work, from processing data to generating insights that inform clinical decisions. Healthcare professionals must also develop data literacy. This isn't merely about collecting data, but interpreting complex datasets to draw meaningful conclusions. Data literacy empowers you to transform raw informa-tion into actionable strategies, enhancing your ability to deliver precise, and effective, care.

Developing comprehensive training programs is the next logical step in equipping healthcare workers with the skills they need to integrate AI into their practice. Workshops on AI tools and software provide hands-on experience with the technologies reshaping healthcare. These sessions offer practical insights into how AI applications can optimize workflows, improve patient outcomes, and reduce errors. Online courses and certifications in AI applications further bolster this learning. These courses offer the flexibility to learn at your own pace, accommodating the busy schedules typical in healthcare settings. You can gain in-depth knowledge of AI's capabilities, applications, and limitations through structured modules, ensuring you are well-prepared for an AI-enhanced environment.

Educational partnerships play a pivotal role in creating tailored AI training programs. Collaborations between healthcare institutions, and universities, can lead to the development of specialized curricula that address the unique needs of the healthcare sector. For example, partnerships with academic institutions can facilitate the design of courses that integrate AI theory with practical applications, ensuring that learning is comprehensive, and relevant. Industry certifications for AI proficiency in healthcare can also validate your skills, and knowledge, enabling you to demonstrate your competence in integrating AI technologies into clinical practice. These certifications testify to your readiness to embrace AI, enhancing your professional credibility, and career prospects.

Training success stories abound, showcasing the transformative impact of well-designed programs. Significant improvements in patient outcomes have been observed in hospitals where comprehensive AI training has been implemented. As an example, healthcare professionals trained in AI-driven diagnostic tools report increased accuracy, leading to more effective treatment plans, and better patient satisfaction. AI literacy programs have also been successful in improving staff engagement, and efficiency. These programs empower healthcare workers to leverage AI insights, optimize workflows, and enhance patient care, by fostering a deeper understanding of AI technologies. These success stories highlight the positive outcomes that can be achieved through targeted training initiatives, demonstrating the value of investing in AI education for healthcare professionals.

Textual Element: Case Study

Consider the example of a large urban hospital implementing a comprehensive AI training program for its staff. Recognizing the transformative potential of AI, the hospital collaborated with a local university to develop a customized curriculum focused on AI applications in healthcare. The program included workshops on AI tools, online modules for self-paced learning, and opportunities for hands-on experience with AI technologies. As a result of this training initiative, hospital staff reported increased confidence in using AI-driven systems, leading to improved diagnostic accuracy, and patient outcomes. The program also fostered a culture of innovation, encouraging staff to explore new ways of integrating AI into their daily practice. This case study illustrates the tangible benefits of investing in AI training for healthcare professionals, underscoring the importance of equipping staff with the skills needed to thrive in an AI-enhanced environment.

This focus on training and development positions healthcare professionals to adapt to, and thrive in, an AI-driven landscape. By prioritizing education and collaboration, healthcare institutions can ensure that their staff are well-equipped to integrate AI technologies into their practice, ultimately enhancing patient care, and improving outcomes. Through targeted training programs, healthcare professionals can build the skills and knowledge necessary to navigate the complexities of AI, empowering them to make informed decisions, and deliver high-quality care, in an increasingly digital world.

3.2 AI and Human Touch: Finding the Balance in Patient Care

In healthcare, human interaction forms the cornerstone of effective patient care. The warmth of a reassuring hand, the soothing tone of a nurse's voice, and the empathetic understanding of a doctor's gaze are irreplaceable. These interactions build trust and rapport, which are essential to a patient's healing journey. Emotional support is often the invisible thread that connects healthcare professionals with their patients, facilitating an environment where patients feel valued, and understood. While AI can provide remarkable insights and efficiencies, it cannot replicate the genuine connection from human empathy. Patients often seek comfort in knowing that their caregivers are not just treating symptoms, but are attuned to their emotional needs. The ability to listen, offer solace during distressing times, and celebrate milestones in recovery are aspects of care that technology cannot replace. Instead, AI's role is to support these interactions, ensuring that healthcare professionals have the time and resources to maintain the human touch that defines compassionate care.

AI is a powerful complement to the human touch, offering tools that enhance patient-centered care. By automating routine tasks, AI liberates healthcare workers from the administrative burdens that often consume their time. This newfound freedom allows professionals to focus more on patient interaction, strengthening the bonds that foster trust, and understanding. AI-driven data analysis further enriches these interactions by providing personalized patient insights. These insights enable healthcare workers to tailor their care approaches, addressing each patient's unique needs and preferences. For instance, AI can analyze a patient's health history, and current data, to suggest customized treatment plans, allowing caregivers to engage in more meaningful discussions about their care options with their patients. Such personalization improves patient outcomes, and reinforces their confidence in their care. The synergy between AI and human touch creates a holistic approach to healthcare, where technology enhances, rather than detracts, from the patient experience.

As AI becomes more prevalent in healthcare, patient concerns about its role in their treatment are natural. Transparency is key in addressing these concerns, ensuring patients feel comfortable, and secure, with AI-assisted care. Clear communication about AI's role in treatment is vital. Patients should understand how AI contributes to their care, what data it analyzes, and how it assists healthcare professionals in making informed decisions. When patients are well-informed, they are more likely to embrace AI as a valuable component of their healthcare. Encouraging patients to participate in discussions about how AI will be used in their treatment, fosters a sense of security, and empowerment. By involving patients in decision-making, healthcare providers can build trust, and alleviate any apprehensions about AI's involvement in their care.

Balancing AI, and human elements in patient care, requires thoughtful strategies to ensure technology enhances the patient's experience. Integrating AI insights into bedside manner is one such strategy. Healthcare professionals can use AI-generated data during patient interactions, providing personalized advice, and recommendations. For example, a doctor might use AI insights to discuss potential lifestyle changes with patients, offering tailored suggestions based on the patient's health data. This integration allows healthcare professionals to provide more informed, and personalized care, while maintaining the personal connection that patients value. Ensuring personal follow-ups alongside AI-generated recommendations is another essential approach. While AI can offer valuable insights, personal interactions remain crucial in reinforcing patient trust, and satisfaction. By following up on AI-driven recommendations with in-person consultations, healthcare professionals can address patients' questions or concerns, ensuring they feel supported, and confident in their care plan.

In the evolving healthcare landscape, finding the balance between AI and human touch is essential. AI can enhance the efficiency and effectiveness of care, but it should always maintain the empathy and compassion that define the human experience. By leveraging AI to support, and improve patient interactions, healthcare professionals can provide the best of both worlds—combining technology's precision with the irreplaceable value of human connection. This harmonious integration of AI, and human touch, promises a future where healthcare is more efficient, compassionate, and patient-centered.

3.3 Future-Ready Skills for Healthcare Professionals

As healthcare continues to evolve with AI integration, professionals must adapt by cultivating skills that are future-ready. The ability to thrive in an AI-driven landscape requires a blend of critical thinking, and problem-solving skills, particularly within AI contexts. Healthcare workers must critically analyze AI-generated data, identify patterns, and make informed decisions that enhance patient care. This skill set empowers you to navigate complex scenarios where AI provides insights, ensuring your clinical judgment remains paramount. Interdisciplinary communication is equally essential, as collaboration across various fields becomes the norm. Engaging with AI specialists, data analysts, and fellow healthcare providers, necessitates clear, effective communication to ensure cohesive care delivery, and innovation. The ability to bridge the gap between technology and healthcare through collaboration, is a defining characteristic of future-ready professionals.

Promoting lifelong learning is crucial in keeping pace with rapid AI advancements. The healthcare industry is dynamic, with continuous innovations shaping how care is delivered. This evolution demands you commit to ongoing education, embracing opportunities to expand your knowledge, and skills. Continuous education opportunities, such as workshops, seminars, and online courses, provide avenues for staying informed about the latest AI developments. These programs enhance your technical proficiency, and broaden your understanding, of AI's potential applications in healthcare. Professional development programs focused on emerging AI technologies offer structured learning experiences that equip you with the tools to adapt to new challenges. By fostering a culture of lifelong learning, healthcare institutions can ensure their staff is well-prepared to leverage AI for improved patient outcomes.

The roles within healthcare are not static; they are evolving in response to AI's influence. New career pathways are emerging in AI-enhanced healthcare, offering opportunities for growth and specialization, as AI becomes more integrated into clinical practice, responsibilities and skill requirements, shift. Healthcare professionals must be adaptable, and ready to embrace new roles aligned with technological advancements. For instance, roles focusing on AI system management, data analysis, and patient engagement through digital platforms are becoming increasingly relevant. These evolving responsibilities require a willingness to learn and adapt, ensuring you remain effective and competitive in a changing landscape. Healthcare professionals can position themselves at the forefront of innovation by exploring new career pathways, and embracing role evolution.

A wealth of skills development resources is available to support this transition. Online AI courses, and certifications, provide flexible learning options, allowing you to acquire new skills quickly. These courses cover a range of topics, from AI fundamentals to specialized applications in healthcare, ensuring that you can tailor your learning to your specific interests and career goals. Workshops, and seminars on emerging healthcare technologies, offer hands-on experience, and insights, from industry experts. These events provide opportunities to network with peers, and learn from leaders in the field, fostering a sense of community and collaboration. By leveraging these resources, healthcare professionals can enhance their knowledge and skills, preparing themselves for the challenges, and opportunities.

Adapting, learning, and collaborating are critical in this rapidly changing environment. By developing future-ready skills, you can navigate the complexities of AI integration, and contribute to a more innovative, patient-centered healthcare system. The journey doesn't end here; it continues as we explore the broader implications of AI on healthcare systems, and the global landscape.

4. Ethical Considerations and Data Privacy

P icture this: a bustling hospital where technology hums quietly in the background, guiding decisions, predicting patient needs, and supporting care teams. In this setting, AI is a silent partner, enhancing the abilities of healthcare professionals to deliver precise and timely care. Yet, as I observed these advancements, a question lingered: How do we ensure this powerful technology serves everyone fairly and ethically? This question is central to the conversation about ethical AI in healthcare. It's about ensuring that AI respects patient rights and upholds the values that underpin our healthcare systems.

Ethical AI in healthcare is guided by several foundational principles, with beneficence and non-maleficence at the forefront. Beneficence refers to the obligation of AI technologies to contribute positively to patient care, enhancing well-being, and improving outcomes. Non-maleficence, on the other hand, mandates that AI systems do not harm, safeguarding patients from potential risks associated with technology use. These principles are complemented by fairness and justice, ensuring that AI algorithms operate without bias, and distribute benefits equitably across all patient groups. This means that AI should not favor one demographic over another, but should provide equal access to its advantages, regardless of socioeconomic status, race, or gender.

Several decision-making frameworks have been developed to navigate the complex landscape of ethical AI implementation. The Asilomar AI Principles offer guidelines for ensuring that AI technologies are aligned with human values, emphasizing transparency, accountability, and the promotion of human welfare. These principles advocate for the responsible development of AI, balancing innovation with ethical considerations. Similarly, the IEEE Global Initiative on Ethics of Autonomous and Intelligent Systems, provides a comprehensive framework for evaluating the moral implications of AI technologies. This initiative stresses the importance of inclusivity, ensuring that diverse perspectives inform the development and deployment, of AI systems (Source 1).

Despite these frameworks, ethical challenges in AI remain pervasive, particularly in healthcare. Informed consent is a critical issue, requiring that patients understand and agree to use AI in their care. This involves communicating how AI technologies will be used, what data they will analyze, and how decisions will be made. Patient autonomy must be respected, allowing individuals to make informed choices about their treatment options. Balancing automation with patient autonomy is another challenge, as AI systems must complement, rather than override, the decision-making capabilities of healthcare professionals. This balance ensures that human judgment remains central to patient care, with AI as a supportive tool, rather than a replacement.

Several case studies illustrate the successful implementation of ethical AI practices in healthcare. In clinical trials, for example, AI is used to maintain participant rights, and ensure ethical standards. By automating data collection and analysis, AI enhances the accuracy and efficiency of trials, while safeguarding participant privacy, and informed consent. Another example is the use of AI in palliative care, where technologies are designed to respect patient dignity and autonomy. AI systems can help manage pain and symptoms, offering personalized care plans that align with the patient's values, and preferences. These applications demonstrate the potential of AI to enhance healthcare delivery while upholding ethical principles.

Textual Element: Reflection Section

Consider the ethical implications of AI in your practice or field. Reflect on how the principles of beneficence, non-maleficence, fairness, and justice could guide the implementation of AI technologies in your work. Consider the decision-making frameworks that could support ethical AI deployment, ensuring patient rights and autonomy are respected. How could you address ethical challenges such as informed consent and balancing automation with human judgment? Reflect on the case studies in this chapter and consider how similar ethical AI practices could be applied in your setting.

As you reflect, consider the following questions: How can you ensure that AI technologies in your field uphold ethical principles, and serve the greater good? What steps could you take to address ethical challenges, and maintain patient trust in AI-driven care? How can you leverage decision-making frameworks, to guide the responsible implementation of AI in your practice?

By exploring these considerations, you can better understand the ethical dimensions of AI in healthcare, and envision how ethical principles can be integrated into your work.

4.1 Navigating Patient Data Privacy in an AI Era

In the rapidly evolving landscape of AI-driven healthcare, protecting patient data privacy has emerged as a critical concern. Integrating AI into healthcare systems offers extraordinary benefits, but also introduces potential risks for data breaches, and unauthorized access to sensitive health information. Imagine a scenario where personal health data entrusted to a healthcare provider falls into the wrong hands. Such breaches can lead to severe consequences, including identity theft, financial loss, and violations of patient confidentiality. Data misuse jeopardizes individual privacy, and erodes trust in healthcare systems, as patients may become reluctant to share vital information necessary for their care.

Legal and regulatory frameworks are pivotal in safeguarding patient data privacy within AI-driven healthcare environments. The Health Insurance Portability and Accountability Act (HIPAA) sets stringent standards for protecting sensitive patient information in the United States. HIPAA regulations require healthcare organizations to implement robust security measures to ensure data confidentiality, integrity, and availability. These regulations mandate authorized individuals access only patient data, with stringent penalties for noncompliance. Meanwhile, the General Data Protection Regulation (GDPR) imposes similar requirements for organizations handling personal data of European Union citizens. GDPR emphasizes explicit consent for data use, minimization, and the right to be forgotten, ensuring that patient data is handled with the utmost care and respect (Source 2).

Healthcare organizations must implement comprehensive data privacy measures to protect patient data in AI systems. Technical solutions, such as data encryption, ensure that sensitive information is securely stored and transmitted, making it difficult for unauthorized parties to access. Encryption converts data into a coded format, requiring a key for decryption, thereby adding a layer of security to patient records. Secure storage solutions, such as cloud-based systems with advanced security protocols, provide additional protection against data breaches. Implementing robust access controls is another crucial strategy, ensuring only authorized personnel can access patient data. Audit trails enhance security by tracking data access and modifications, enabling organizations to monitor and respond to unauthorized activities swiftly.

Emerging privacy-preserving technologies offer innovative approaches to safeguarding patient data while allowing AI innovation to flourish. Differential privacy is a technique designed to protect individual privacy by adding a certain degree of noise to datasets. This method ensures that the data analysis output does not reveal any specific individual's information, allowing researchers to gain insights from data without compromising privacy. Federated learning presents another promising solution, enabling decentralized data processing. This approach trains AI models across multiple devices without transferring raw data to a central server. Instead, only the model updates are shared, ensuring that sensitive data remains on local devices. This decentralized method enhances data privacy while maintaining the benefits of collective learning, offering a balanced approach to leveraging AI in healthcare.

AI and data privacy intersection is dynamic, and requires ongoing vigilance and adaptation. As AI technologies advance, so must the strategies and frameworks that protect patient data. By prioritizing data privacy, and implementing robust security measures, healthcare organizations can harness the power of AI to improve patient outcomes, while maintaining the trust and confidence of those they serve.

4.2 Addressing Algorithmic Bias in Healthcare Applications

When computers learn from data that's not entirely fair, it can affect the health care you receive, and worsen existing problems. This is often because the information used to teach the computer models is not balanced, or doesn't represent all the people healthcare services look after. For example, if the data is mostly from one group of people, the computer model might work well for them, but not as well for others. This happened in the Framingham Heart Study, where the computer found heart disease risk more precisely in Caucasians, compared to African Americans. Such unfairness can make the computer give advice that isn't right for everyone, making the computer's help in health, less fair and reliable. Unfair computer models can have significant effects, especially in patient care. They can lead to wrong diagnoses, and suggest wrong treatments, meaning some people get worse care, or miss out on the right treatments. This can worsen existing healthcare issues, especially for groups already struggling to get good care. On top of this, these unfair situations can lead to unequal access to improvements in computer technology, further widening the gap in healthcare outcomes. More and more, healthcare depends on computers, so these issues are not only technical, but also ethical, and need to be resolved fast. To handle this unfairness, we need to start with the data. The information that teaches computer models must represent everyone equally. We must include data from many groups so our computers can learn about everyone's unique health needs. Regular checks for unfairness are also helpful, which involves reviewing the computer systems, and correcting them. Assessments can help find any unfairness in the computer's predictions, making developers refine their models to make them fair. This recurrent process of checks and adjustments helps ensure our computer models are fair, and effective for everyone.

Several groups have made great strides in lessening bias in algorithms, creating valuable takeaways for use in healthcare. For instance, some AI developers build tools to find, and solve, bias in their systems. These tools closely monitor AI results, spotting, and fixing, any bias immediately. By doing this, AI systems can always stay fair, and adjust to different patient needs. United efforts to make algorithms more straightforward have also worked well. By teaming up, healthcare providers, tech experts, and researchers, can swap knowledge and plans for shrinking bias, helping to create a culture of responsibility, and ongoing progress. These combined efforts allow for sharing the best ways to do things, and setting rules for using AI ethically in healthcare.

Fixing bias in an algorithm is a complicated but essential job in healthcare's constantly changing world of AI. As we continue, the dedication to fairness and equality in AI will become vital in unlocking all the benefits these technologies can offer. By focusing on diversity, clarity, and collaboration, we can create AI systems that improve healthcare results for everyone, ensuring every patient can benefit from technological advances.

4.3 Building Trust: Ensuring Transparency and Fairness

Healthcare trust is key for patients and doctors to connect effectively. When AI technology is used more in hospitals, and clinics, people need to know how that technology works, otherwise, it could lead to misunderstanding, and people not trusting it. In AI, being transparent means telling people how they make decisions. For instance, if patients understand how AI decides what's wrong with them, they're more likely to believe it. The same goes for doctors. If they know what the AI can do, it's easier for them to use it in their work. That helps everyone work better, together, with AI technology assisting doctors to give the proper care to their patients. Just as important is letting people know what AI can't do. This sets the right expectations, and stops people from relying too much on AI, beyond what it can do now. Being honest builds trust where patients, and doctors, are sure that AI is useful in healthcare. Equally important is that everyone has access to these AI tools – not just some people. No matter how much money people have, or where they live, they should all be able to use AI systems. This requires ensuring AI technology is available every-where, from more wealthy areas to less advantaged places. To make the benefits of AI more equal, you must understand, and reduce, the things that limit people from getting to these technologies. For exam-ple, healthcare organizations could implement policies to give resources to less privileged communities. By doing this, AI can help improve healthcare results for all kinds of patients, making things fairer. Fairness also includes the results from AI applications. The AI's decisions should be consistent for all patients, and not favor one group. To make this happen, AI has to be checked, and improved, to give everyone the best results, regardless of their background, or situation.

Building the trust of everyone involved in creating, and using AI in health care is essential. It's key that patients have a say regarding how AI will impact their treatment. Patients' thoughts, and worries, can help shape AI systems to suit their needs better. By including patients right from the start, healthcare centers show they're all for transparency, and inclusion. This helps make patients feel they're part of the process, and trust it more. Teaming up with groups that speak for patients adds to this effort. These groups offer critical viewpoints on what different patient groups need, and their rights. This teamwork can help create AI systems that are not just clever, but good for society, in other words, socially responsible, and match up with what the communities they're helping care about. Healthcare centers that are open and fair have implemented different projects to build trust in AI. For instance, some explain how their AI models work, explaining their methods, and the information they use. This openness means others can check the accuracy of their work. Public meetings that explain AI are another way of building trust. These meetings help the public understand AI better, dispelling any myths, and dealing with any concerns they may have. They are also a good place for patients, and healthcare professionals, to learn more about AI, and what it means for the future in the medical field. By doing all this, healthcare centers are creating a feeling of trust and teamwork, painting AI as a helper, rather than something to be feared. In short, being open and fair is the best way to build trust in healthcare AI. Openly talking about AI, ensuring everyone can use it, and getting everyone involved, can help healthcare centers create a place where people trust AI. This trust is essential for AI to work well, and help make health care better.

5. AI-Powered Innovations in Patient Care

Picture a world where a visit to your doctor's office is as unique as your fingerprint, and all treatments are tailor-made, just for you. They consider the current state of your health, your genetic make-up, and how you live your life. This is what personalized medicine promises. AI techniques are making this exciting idea a reality, which means personalized medicine changes patient care forever. It goes from a "one-size-fits-all" style, to a treatment plan made for each individual patient, using their genetic details to create the best treatment plans. AI also helps in creating medicines that match those details perfectly. This precision means your doctor's visits will be as perfect, and effective, as possible. Proper treatment can reduce harmful effects, and improve the good ones. Simply, AI helps make medicine more personal. This same AI can examine patient data in great detail, using smart ways to make very precise treatment plans. It accounts for various things, like your genes, past diseases, and lifestyle. As an example, AI checks your chance of getting certain diseases, which allows doctors to take steps, before a problem starts. It can spot patterns in your data, catching ominous signs early, which allows doctors to help, before things get too bad. AI also matches therapies to patient history, and preferences. This way, treatments fit your health needs, and personal values, putting you at the center of your care. You'll be able to make better choices about your health, which means better results, and satisfaction with your care.

There are many examples of AI working well in personalized medicine, one key example being Oncology care. AI has helped create targeted treatments, and improved patient results, by finding specific changes that lead to cancer, looking at a patient's genes. This lets doctors pick treatments that target these changes, killing the cancer, without harming healthy tissue. Analyzing data from body monitors, and patient files, AI can provide dietary changes, and exercise programs. It can also make you as healthy as possible, and help prevent the development of long-term diseases. These exciting changes show how AI healthcare can meet patients' unique needs, allowing for a more proactive, and preventive way, of approaching medicine. Simply put, AI is the future of how we take care of ourselves.

Even though personalized healthcare, powered by AI, will change the world of medicine, it's not an easy thing to implement. One big hurdle is combining health data from multiple sources, so all your health information is in one place for easy review, working best for everyone. To accomplish this, there needs to be a strong system setup, as well as rules, to easily share, and use data, across many platforms. Another issue is ensuring patients understand what's happening. Because tech analyzes their personal data, it's important they know how that information will be used, and feel comfortable it's secure. You mustn't be left in the dark about anything, not just for trust's sake, but also to ensure your privacy is respected, and absolute. Despite these hurdles, AI in medicine will do a lot of good, and enhance how we handle patient care. By sorting out data issues, and hearing the patient's voice, doctors can use AI to its fullest potential, which in turn helps them provide excellent care for each patient. These new tech innovations are making healthcare more about individual needs, and a better, more efficient system, where every treatment is designed specifically for them. This is a massive step towards a patient-focused healthcare system where AI can give you the best health outcome possible.

5.1 AI in Surgery: Precision and Safety Enhancements

AI-powered tech is making a massive difference in surgeries. Have you heard of robotic surgical systems, like the da Vinci? They are bringing about significant change in how surgeries are performed. With their robotic arms, they perform strict tasks, guided by experienced surgeons, who control them from a console. It translates their hand movements to precise actions on the patient's body. This helps in doing delicate tasks, better than any traditional methods, decreasing mistakes, and increasing the surgeon's ability. The results are fewer complications, and quicker patient recovery. As more minor cuts are made, these less invasive techniques aid in faster healing, and shorter hospital stays. In addition, AI-enhanced imaging takes surgical precision to a whole new level, giving real-time, ultra clear images, allowing surgeons to move through complex body structures with confidence. The tech identifies important structures, and potential risks, reducing the chances of damaging the surrounding tissues. When doing complicated surgeries, like on the brain, AI-assisted imaging helps find tumor locations with pinpoint accuracy. This lets surgeons remove tumors precisely, without harming healthy brain tissue. Patients have fewer complications after surgery, and a better quality of life, because important functions are protected. However, the use of AI in surgeries isn't just about precision, it also supports less invasive techniques. These techniques create more minor cuts, leading to less pain, less scarring, and a lower risk of infection. Patients recover faster, getting back to their daily lives sooner. AI also helps plan, and execute surgeries, using pre-surgery data that suggests the optimal approach. Surgeons can practice the surgery beforehand, tackling possible issues, and sharpening their strategies. All these steps reduce the chance of any surprises occurring during a surgery, ensuring smoother operations, and better patient outcomes.

AI helps doctors with surgeries, making them even better at what they do. For example, during joint replacement, AI can help position the implants just right, making the joint last longer, and work better. This can also help patients move around more easily, and experience less discomfort. AI also makes its mark in brain surgery - it can analyze complex scans, and make it easier for surgeons to single out, and remove tumors while, keeping the healthy surrounding tissues unharmed. This proves AI's usefulness for surgical precision and safety, all for the patient's good. However, introducing AI in surgery is not all smooth sailing. There's a lot to think about concerning ethics, and practical matters. Surgeons must receive sound training in operating AI systems correctly, to use the technology effectively. Patients must fully understand AI's role in their surgeries, including all the possible advantages, and disadvantages. Explaining everything clearly can help build trust with their surgeons, and enable patients to make informed choices about their treatment. There are also ethical issues to consider, like who's responsible if something goes wrong during surgery - is it the machine, the doctor, or both? Clear regulations can help solve this problem, by outlining who's accountable for what happens. Then there's the question of data privacy, because AI systems need a lot of patient data to work effectively. Keeping this information secure, helps build patient trust. We can keep patient data confidential by following the rules and regulations, and using strong security measures.

AI is getting better every day. It might even with help more surgeries soon, improving patient care, but first, we must consider how to use AI properly, and fairly. By doing so, hospitals can help more people, and make surgeries better and safer for their patients.

5.2 Virtual Health Assistants: Guiding Patients Remotely

Virtual health assistants are like superheroes in a digital world, revolutionizing the way we look after our health! They're super smart, AI-powered buddies, always there to help you care for yourself, no matter where you are. Think of them as a digital nurse, or doctor, at your fingertips. These digital helpers come in many different forms! Some might chat with you in real time, answering your health questions, or guiding you down the right path. Others could be like virtual nurse buddies, helping you manage long-term health issues. If you have diabetes, for example, an assistant could set insulin reminders, make meal suggestions, even help you understand your blood sugar levels. However, they're not just robotic voices—they really get you. They're designed to understand what you as a patient need, making sure you get the proper care and support, just like you would if you were talking to a real person. These virtual health assistants have a ton of perks, especially when it comes to making healthcare more accessible. The best part is they're always there, day or night, so you can get help, anytime you need it. This round-the-clock support takes a load off health centers' plates, and puts control of your health, directly into your own hands. Another exciting thing they do is give personalized health tips, and reminders, sifting through your health data, and providing targeted advice for managing your health more effectively. This becomes handy if you have a chronic condition, because you get constant guidance, which can dramatically improve your health. In addition, with these helpers dealing with everyday tasks like data analysis, doctors and nurses can focus their attention on more significant health concerns. There have been some serious success stories with these AI assistants. Patients with diabetes, for example, have managed their blood sugar levels better with the help of AI coaches. The assistants provide them with regular feedback, and adjust to their habits, making managing the disease easier by reducing the chances of complications. They've also made enormous strides in mental health care, by offering a platform that's private, and easy to reach for anyone needing support. Virtual counselors chat with users, check on their moods and symptoms, and provide ways to cope. Such experiences highlight how virtual assistants can improve individual health, and make healthcare more efficient, by letting care reach beyond hospital, or clinic, walls.

Virtual health helpers can be tricky to create, and have certain limits. One big issue is ensuring they work well for all users. This means considering different ages, tech skills and languages, to give everyone a positive experience. Building trust is also very important, as users need to know that their private data is safe and, the information they receive is correct. Open and honest communication about how virtual health helpers work, what info they collect, and how they use it, is critical in helping users feel more at ease. To get the most from virtual health helpers, it's important to figure out these issues. This is because for them to work best, users need to be involved, and completely comfortable with them. As virtual health helpers get better, they have the potential to change the way we see healthcare. Their knack for reliable, tailored help, could make users more independent, and healthier overall. When used correctly in the healthcare system, these digital tools may preview a time when good healthcare reaches everyone, no matter where they live.

5.3 Predictive Analytics in Proactive Healthcare Management

Healthcare is getting better, thanks to "predictive analytics", a tool that helps foresee patients' needs, like having a crystal ball! What this means is doctors can guess what a patient needs, before anything bad happens. Predictive analytics use past data, unique formulas, and machine learning, to make these guesses, helping to show what happens to health in the future. It's an essential tool for healthcare, putting patient care a step ahead, so doctors can do something before health worsens. Early warning systems help a lot, too. They warn doctors if a patient isn't doing well, so the doctor can be pre-active. Real-time data, like vital signs and lab results, tell the system if a patient's health is about to decline. These systems make healthcare better, because they raise alarms early. In this way, doctors can sort out problems, before they grow too big. It helps people stay healthier, and go to the hospital less. Predictive analytics are invaluable for managing long-term illnesses, too. They use data from electronic health records, health monitors, and past health information, to determine who is more susceptible to long-term illnesses, like diabetes, or high blood pressure. By finding these people, doctors can help prevent the illness from starting, or slow it down if it already has. It changes healthcare from only treating symptoms, or illnesses, to preventing health problems from happening at all. Predictive analytics has many uses in healthcare. It helps improve patient care, and health results. It's helpful when doctors try to determine which patients might return to the hospital soon. By looking at things like past stays, other illnesses, and life conditions, they know who to focus on. Doctors can plan better, make personalized plans when patients leave the hospital, and check up on patients after they leave. These things can prevent patients from returning to the hospital, and feel much better about their care. Furthermore, healthcare locations can guess how many patients will come, and plan accordingly, ensuring they have enough staff to care for patients in the best way possible.

Healthcare has been revolutionized by introducing predictive analytics. The program assists in swiftly helping patients based on their symptoms, past medical issues, and vital signs. This tool is fast, reduces waiting time, and ensures the most urgent cases are seen to, immediately. We have also seen great results detecting sepsis earlier. Sepsis, a severe reaction to infection, requires rapid treatment to avoid life-threatening complications. The software has revealed patterns in patients' health data, warning early of the onset of sepsis, however, implementing such powerful tools in healthcare isn't without its challenges. It's crucial to have good quality, comprehensive datasets, after all, the tool's reliability depends on the accuracy of the data. Inadequate or biased data might result in wrong predictions, threatening the patient's well-being. To overcome these issues, organizations must invest in a strong data management system that can vouch for the data's quality and wholeness. Another hurdle is ensuring the predictions are incorporated into everyday clinical practice. Doctors and nurses need to be trained to understand these insights, and use them wisely in their decisions. This means a massive change among healthcare staff, as they learn to trust, and act on, these data-based insights in conjunction with their clinical experience.

Summing up, predictive analytics is indeed a beacon, lighting up the path to a more proactive, and efficient, healthcare system. It uses data to understand patients' needs, and prevent severe situations. This method improves results, relieves the system, and makes healthcare more affordable and accessible. Our next chapter will explore the ethical concerns and challenges of using AI in healthcare. We will examine the responsibilities of integrating these potent technologies into patient care.

6. Investment and Market Trends in Healthcare AI

P icture yourself walking into a busy room full of excited investors, all searching for the hottest new thing in healthcare tech, and can't wait to hear about new AI ideas that could change how we care for patients. You are amazed by how AI has quickly become a key part of investing in healthcare. In this part, we explore how technology and money interact closely in this field. This will give you valuable knowledge to understand this changing world.

6.1 Evaluating AI Technologies: A Guide for Investors

Healthcare AI is constantly changing, and it's important for those investing, to understand the basics. AI programs, like supervised and unsupervised learning, are used in a variety of ways in healthcare, helping predict outcomes, and monitor patients. Supervised learning uses classified data to guide predictions, which is handy for diagnostic tools. Unsupervised learning finds patterns in data, without any preset categories. This is great for uncovering new connections in patient data. The strength and trustworthiness of AI are vital, as they work better with top-notch, varied data. Quality data lets AI make correct guesses, while different data types reduce bias, and prevent skewed results. Investors should look for companies dedicated to high data standards, and ongoing improvement. Seeing whether AI tech can work in the market involves studying things like demand, potential for growth, and competition. The healthcare AI market is growing fast, and more places are seeing how AI can improve patient care. Still, competition is tough. New companies need to show why they're different, and better. For example, startups that use already-existing systems for things like health records, have an easier time fitting in. This puts them at an advantage in the market. Another key factor is scalability. Tech should be able to handle more significant operations, without losing quality. Investors should look for companies with a track record of growth, without compromising their AI products. The way AI healthcare companies do business also affects investing prospects. Many operate using a "software-as-a-service model". This offers cloud-based solutions that are flexible, and easy to grow. Healthcare providers can use advanced AI tools, without needing much on-site equipment, which reduces cost, and speeds up deployment. Licensing and subscription models also exist. These provide steady income, and foster loyal customers. The proper pricing and value balance is essential to ensure clients benefit from their investment. Understanding how business models fit market needs, and client expectations, is vital for investors to gauge possible returns.

Healthcare AI is a big deal, but we must think hard about how it works, and whether it's doing the right thing. First, it must always work well, no matter what. If it messes up, people's health can be at risk, which we can't allow. Second, we need to think about what's right and wrong. Using AI in healthcare raises issues about keeping patient data safe, respecting privacy, and if patients will agree to its use. Investors need to check if companies are taking these challenges seriously. They must ensure companies follow the rules, and meet everyone's expectations. If it does a good job with these things, doctors and patients are more likely to trust, and support them.

Fun Task for Investors

- Get acquainted with AI magic: Learn about cool AI tricks that are helping healthcare developers.
- Aim for top-notch data: Look for companies that use different, top-quality data.
- Research the popularity: Check if AI tools are wanted, can grow, and win competitions.
- Get to know the businesses: See if subscription methods fit the market's desires.
- Define fairness: Make sure companies are working on keeping patient info safe, and handling data correctly.

In the exciting world of AI in healthcare, smart investors have a chance. They can back up remarkable technologies that help patients, make healthcare more efficient, and advance medical research. How? By looking closely at the tech details, market trends, how a business makes money, and important ethical matters. This puts you in a good spot to invest in a way that makes you money, and makes real progress in healthcare.

6.2 Emerging Trends: The Next Frontier in Healthcare AI

AI is doing some seriously cool stuff in the health world. It's making drug discoveries faster and cheaper, which means life-saving medicines can reach patients sooner. Here's how it works: AI uses machine learning to find possible drugs quickly. It's much faster than the traditional way - no long years or tons of money needed. The AI scans large piles of data to find promising chemicals. It can also predict how a new drug might work by looking at patterns in chemical structures and how they interact with the body. This not only speeds up getting medicines to patients but also reduces costs, so more people can access treatments. With AI, we can tackle complex diseases better and bring hope for conditions that haven't yet seen effective treatment. That's not all. AI can also bleach our genetic codes, helping us better understand diseases. This can advance personalized medicine – where treatments are arranged to suit each person's genetic makeup. The AI quickly analyzes piles of genetic data to find signs linked to specific diseases. This helps in making targeted therapies that work better and are much safer. It's the same with proteins - AI helps understand their structures and what they do, essential for understanding diseases and finding new treatment methods. With the help of AI, we're getting better at diagnosing and treating diseases. It's moving us toward a health system that can prevent illness before it starts.

In the health industry, significant changes are happening because of new AI technology. This is especially true when thinking about personalized medicine and telehealth. Personalized medicine is not just an idea from the future anymore. With AI, treatments can suit each person's health needs. AI can take information from different places, like digital health records or fitness trackers, to make a complete health outline of a person. This new approach turns a person's health care plan from just responding to diseases to being proactive in preventing them. Telehealth is also growing, and AI is helping it. Remote check-ups are improving, and people are finding it easier to connect with their healthcare providers. AI makes it simple for patients and doctors to communicate, helping with virtual consultations in an efficient way. This is particularly useful for people in isolated or under-supported areas, giving them access to health care without traveling. Looking ahead, the future of AI in healthcare is promising. This is especially true for mental health care and home health care services. AI is being used more and more to help with mental health problems. Some tools can detect early warning signs, create personalized treatment plans, and give ongoing support. For example, AI-powered chat programs and virtual therapists make professional mental health care more available to people. Doing this makes it easier for people to get the help they need and reduces the stigma around seeking treatment. As a result, there is expected to be a lot of growth in AI services for mental health care. In the same way,

AI is helping to grow home healthcare services. This changes how health care can be given and allows people to get high-quality care from the comfort of their own homes. With AI, doctors can monitor a person's well-being by checking vital signs and health data. They can then warn healthcare providers about possible issues before they become big problems. This proactive approach improves the patient's health and removes pressure from regular healthcare facilities.

Sure, AI can do some amazing things in healthcare, but it's not all smooth sailing. There are hurdles to jump, like proving that AI's decisions are transparent and easy-to-understand for doctors and patients alike. This 'tell me how you did it' part is significant because it builds faith in AI and 'healthcare helpers' and ensures they work as needed. Plus, with AI getting brainier daily, faster and stronger gadgets and systems are required to keep up. As AI gets better, so does the demand for high-power tech. Building this super tech is a must if we want to see AI go far in healthcare. These tech upgrades will be key to beating challenges and showing what AI can do to change how we look after our health.

6.3 Case Studies: Successful AI Investments in Healthcare

AI businesses are making huge moves in the healthcare world, and many investments are changing the game. A great example is when people put money into AI startups that help diagnose diseases, and change how we find, and deal with them. One such startup made an AI system that can understand radiological images, better than people can. Investors saw the promise in this startup early on. They noted how technology can cut down mistakes in diagnoses, and help make treatment decisions quicker. This investment pushed the startup to the front lines of diagnosing diseases, and showed the importance of matching AI skills with urgent healthcare needs. There are also many successful partnerships between AI companies, and healthcare institutions. Imagine a situation where a well-known AI company worked with a top hospital, and combined AI to predict patient care. This partnership lets data be analyzed, in real time, to guide doctors' decisions. This decreased the number of patients who had to come back for treatment, and made the results better for them. Those who invested in this venture understood the strength of working together. They saw that groundbreaking AI technology, and deep-rooted healthcare structures, can give powerful results when combined. Therefore, such investments aren't just about technology, they're also about building strong ties that strengthen AI pioneers, and healthcare providers.

People who invest well in healthcare AI, often use methods that weigh the risks, against the potential gains. They skillfully take on tricky situations with this knowledge, and invest in varying AI technologies, to spread out risk, and make profits from different innovation lines. For example, an investor might put money into multiple AI tools that can diagnose, or cure diseases. By hedging their bets, they can lessen the damage, if something goes wrong in any one area. The choice between long-term and short-term investment choices can shape what happens. Long-term investments let AI technologies grow over time, which suits how they develop, and are accepted by the market. On the other hand, short-term investments might give quick returns, but they often need precise market timing, and the ability to spot new trends. These examples provide crucial lessons for future investment choices in healthcare AI. One big lesson is that it's vital to do your homework, and understand the market, before investing. Knowing about the competition, regulations, and whether the technology will work, can help make wise and lasting investment decisions. Another significant point is understanding how essential it is to create strong relationships, and connections. Working with healthcare organizations, tech providers, and rule-makers, can offer insights and resources that strengthen the success, and power, of AI investments. Sharing knowledge, and encouraging an innovation-rich environment, can push the whole sector forward.

Venture capital is key to growth, and new ideas, in healthcare AI. When venture capitalists invest early in a startup, they can shape its destiny, helping refine the tech for the market. Venture capitalists offer money, mentorship, industry contacts, and strategic advice, which is priceless for young companies. However, venture capital's influence doesn't stop at one company - it affects the healthcare sector's AI approach. By investing in promising AI solutions, venture capitalists help get them into actual medical practice faster. This improves patient care, and makes operations more efficient. The give-and-take between venture capital, and AI innovation, is a great example of how money know-how, excellent planning, and working together, can take healthcare to new heights. As the AI field grows, we'll take the lessons from these investments forward. They'll inform money-making strategies while also helping healthcare improve for everyone.

6.4 Navigating Market Risks: Informed Investment Decisions

Putting money into healthcare's AI tech is like walking a tightrope. You need to know what you're doing. Rules? They're everywhere. To keep patients safe, and ensure new tech works, healthcare has some strict regulations in place. Getting a "yes" to new AI tech can take time and money, slowing things down for investors. So, if you're looking to invest, you need to keep a sharp eye on these rules, and know what's needed for AI. Chatting with people who know all about it can give you some helpful pointers, and highlight any hurdles early on. You also need to think about tech going out of date quickly, because of AI's fast-paced advances. If better algorithms and systems emerge, what's new and exciting today, could be old news tomorrow. Investors must keep tabs on tech trends, and be ready for twists and turns, that could hit their investments. So, how do you tackle these risks? One word - diversification. Just like with regular investments, spreading your cash across different types of AI tech can lower your risk if one falls through. In this way, you can handle the risk, but still be part of the significant gains in the sector. Teaming up with rule experts and advisors, can also help crack the code of compliance. These pros can guide you in the rules, and future healthcare AI changes. This advice is golden – it means you can ensure your investments match today's, and tomorrow's standards.

Shaky markets can affect AI healthcare spending. Changing money situations, new health policies, and different tech trends, can change how much money is available, and what AI firms are worth. To manage these changes, those who invest money need to plan for these money factors affecting AI funding. Grasping key economic signs, and their effect on investment, can aid these investors in more intelligent decision-making. In addition, thinking long-term can offer a secure feeling, letting investors ride out the rough times, and take advantage of recovery periods. Making your investment list strong against these ups and downs is essential for continued success in the AI health market. More than just money, moral and societal effects matter as well, when investing. Putting money into AI projects that benefit society, combines financial goals with moral duties. This means backing tech that betters patient care, boosts health access, and tackles health result differences. Mixing profit with ethical thoughts isn't just about doing what's right; it also shapes how the public sees and trusts you.

Businesses with a focus on doing what is right often get more support. This support can come from shoppers, health experts, and official groups. People who want to invest their money should look for chances that align with what is important to them. They should know that investing money responsibly, can help improve the money return, and benefit society. As we finish this part, the details of putting money into health AI should be precise. By knowing the risks, creating ways to reduce them, thinking about market changes, and the right things to do, you can make knowledgeable choices that help the sector grow, and create new things. Looking ahead, we will explore the rules and policies that shape the future of AI in healthcare, and how these areas affect the use, and fitting in of AI technologies, in the industries.

7. Regulatory and Policy Considerations

E nvision a world where AI becomes a permanent part of every area in healthcare, making patient care better, and safer. While this future is exciting, it's also tricky. We must follow many rules, and policies, to ensure these AI systems are secure and valuable. It's like finding your way through a maze to bring AI from an idea, to an accurate tool in healthcare. At each turn, we must think carefully about the regulations controlling our use of AI. These rules aren't just jumping through hoops—they're essential shields to protect patients, and improve health services. One key player in these rules is the Food and Drug Administration, (FDA), in the United States. The FDA gives guidelines for AI health devices. They ensure these devices are safe and effective, before they reach the market. This includes a thorough before-market approval process. During this process, creators must give detailed research that proves their AI tools work well, and are safe to use in clinics. They must also do a lot of testing to ensure the AI tools don't add new dangers to patient care. If creators follow these rules, they can win the trust of health professionals and patients. These are the people who depend on AI for essential health choices.

The European Medicines Agency, (EMA), works like the US in Europe, as they enforce the EU Medical Device Regulation (MDR). This rule keeps an eye on healthcare AI apps, but the EMA isn't just about sticking to the rules. They also want to help innovation grow, while maintaining safety at the top of their list. They have a big five-year plan for AI, that emphasizes how necessary it is to all work together; training people in all aspects, and trying new things, in the fast-growing world of AI (Source 2). Regular talks with stakeholders, and rules updates, ensure they keep up with tech growth. These steps are key to finding the right balance between pushing for more innovation, and protecting public health. Sticking to these rules can be a pain for the people developing AI, and also for the healthcare providers themselves. Getting approval for AI tools can take a lot of resources, and often needs a lot of evidence, and documentation, proving they're doing everything by the book. This can cause stress between the need for fresh ideas, and staying within the confines of oversight. Developers must figure out how to work in a world where rules are constantly evolving, and can slow down, or change the process, of creating and rolling out AI tech. To stay on top of things, they need a solid game plan. This includes constantly checking for rule updates, and speaking with rule makers to address possible issues.

Clinical trial needs can make AI-focused solutions more complex. These tests are needed to ensure AI tools work safely, and well, in the real world, however, they can be complex, and challenging to design correctly. They must consider peculiar things about healthcare settings, and accurately measure AI's performance. Makers of these tools must ensure that test designs are strong and all-inclusive, recording data showcasing the varied patient groups, and healthcare settings where AI will be used. This calls for teamwork between toolmakers, healthcare workers, and regulatory bodies, setting clear goals, and ways for testing AI solutions. Handling compliance isn't impossible; it just needs careful thought, and teamwork. Toolmakers, and healthcare workers, must understand the complex parts of regulatory frameworks together, using their knowledge, and skill, to ensure that AI tools pass the highest safety and quality checks. This would mean balancing innovation with regulations, and providing new-age AI solutions within rules. By communicating clearly with regulatory bodies, and continuously talking to each other, they can handle any possible issues, and make sure AI fits into healthcare systems successfully.

Textual Element: Key Compliance Checklist

- Learn the rules: Know the FDA and EMA's guidelines for AI medical devices.
- Ready for Market: Show solid evidence that your product is safe and effective.
- Plan Solid Trials: Work closely with healthcare providers to ensure tests reflect real-life situations.
- Talk To Authorities: Keep the lines of communication open to get the latest updates on regulations.
- Mix Creativity and Rules: Plan your development goals per regulatory standards.

So, what's this all about? Well, it's pretty simple. If manufacturers stick to these rules, they won't get lost in the tricky laws and regulations surrounding AI tech. In doing so, their AI tools will be compliant, helping to make healthcare safer, and work better for everyone. It's a win-win!

We'd Love to Hear Your Thoughts on *AI In Healthcare*!

AI is transforming healthcare in incredible ways, making patient care faster, smarter, and safer. Like any significant journey, it's full of challenges and breakthroughs. In *AI In Healthcare*, V. Soltis explores how artificial intelligence is reshaping medicine, and what it means for the future of healthcare.

Why Your Review Matters

Here's where you come in! Your voice matters, and your feedback can help other readers discover the value of this book.

Your thoughts can make a big difference! Reviews help others decide if this book is right for them, and inspire more conversations about the exciting potential of AI in healthcare. In addition, we'd love to know what you enjoyed most, or how the book inspired your perspective on AI, and medicine.

How to Leave a Review

- Head over to the book's page on Amazon, Goodreads, or wherever you got your copy.
- Write a few sentences sharing what stood out to you—maybe it was the easy-to-follow explanations, the real-life examples, or the exciting look at what's next for AI in health.
- Click submit, and you're done!

What to Include

- What did you like best about the book?
- Did it help you understand AI's role in healthcare?
- Would you recommend it to someone curious about technology in medicine?

Every review, big or small, helps! Thank you for taking a moment to share your thoughts on *AI In Healthcare*. Together, we can spread the word about the exciting ways AI is shaping the future of healthcare. Thank you for your time, we look forward to hearing what you think.

7.1 Policy Formulation: Incorporating AI in Healthcare Systems

Making policies that easily mix AI into health systems needs care. The first job is to set clear aims. The people making the policies must spell out what they want AI to do. It could be making patient results better, making operations smoother, or making research better. These aims should go hand in hand with broader health goals, and rules. Chatting with people from all areas, like health providers, tech makers, and patients, is key. This will ensure that the policies are suitable for all. When everyone is involved, they feel part of it, making working together easier, which helps AI to be smoothly introduced. Policymakers should encourage partnerships between public groups, and private businesses. These partnerships can spark new ideas, and help make AI solutions that fit health needs. By joining resources, and expert knowledge, these partnerships can accelerate the use of AI tools, and systems. Policymakers can also push research and development rewards to inspire new ideas. Giving tax cuts, or grants, can get companies excited about doing AI research, creating breakthroughs that were once thought impossible. These incentives can also lure top-skilled people, and breed a space of creativity and discovery. This is fundamentally needed for the growth of AI in healthcare.

Looking at real examples of well-executed plans can teach us a lot. Some countries, like the UK and Canada, have made nationwide plans for AI, and show us how important it is to work together. These plans often involve teamwork, putting money into resources, and thinking about ethics. For example, the UK's AI plan points out the need for data to work across systems, and keep patients safe. It ensures AI is not just new, but also secure, and doing its job. Smaller, local plans can also work well, and lets places sort out healthcare problems that matter most to them. Sometimes, it might mean using AI in public health projects, wherein other times, it could mean making hospitals work better. There can be roadblocks when trying to put AI plans into action. These often come from people in healthcare being scared to shake things up. Workers might worry about losing their jobs, or the new systems may be too complicated, which can make them slow to use AI. To get past this, we must be honest about why AI is there to aid, not replace, them. Training, and workshops, can help workers see how great AI is, and teach them to use it effectively. Another significant roadblock is making sure plans can change with new technology. AI is constantly growing, and if plans are too strict, they can be left behind. People who make plans should create ones that can adapt. They should keep learning from how AI is being used, and implement new research. That way, the plans stay useful, and encourage new ideas, rather than stopping them.

Bringing AI into health systems means more than just using new tech, it's about building a place where new ideas can grow. We must involve everyone to make AI work well, build strong teams, and support research. How other countries have done well with AI can teach us a lot. We must also tackle problems like people's resistance to change, and strict policies. In this way, we make a sturdy plan that helps AI fit into healthcare. Additionally, this kind of plan improves how we care for patients, and readies health systems for whatever comes next.

7.2 Bridging Gaps: Collaborating with Policy Makers

In the ever-changing world of healthcare, it's essential that healthcare providers, tech creators, and those who make the rules, work together closely. This is imperative for making AI work in the best way possible. This team effort isn't nice, but it's a must-have because AI is tricky, and needs multiple brains to get it right. Bringing many different ideas to the table, by forming a kind of "super team", they can focus on making AI the best it can be. This also means their rules will be well thought out, and won't leave anyone out. The team can develop shared goals, smooth out any wrinkles, and tackle problems from the start, making certain there's a good plan for fitting AI into the whole system. Workshops, and forums, where everyone can talk, and share ideas, are needed. These meetings help ensure no question goes unanswered, and everyone has a voice. People can express their worries in these friendly meeting places, chat about what could happen, and suggest new ideas. Having conversations that include everyone is essential for dealing with their worries, and insures they're all on the same page regarding the AI projects. Regular meetings, and chats, let healthcare providers, tech creators, and rule makers, know what's new, so they can align their efforts. These meetups are perfect for talking about changes in the rules, and new tech that's been developed, ensuring everyone agrees. Making a way for the rule makers to hear from others, is also essential for continued improvement. Actively asking for other people's thoughts, rulemakers can see where changes may be needed, and use the information to improve their approach. This ongoing conversation provides clarification, helps build trust within the team, and ensures AI projects stay focused, and realistic. By keeping this conversation open, the group can work together to overcome any hurdles, adapt to change, and successfully create a plan for using AI tech.

Successful team projects provide helpful lessons in creating, and implementing, strong AI rules. Collaborations between private business, and government, improve AI research and its uses. These partnerships help accelerate advancements, and make it easier to implement new technology. Both teams use their strong points to give top-of-the-line answers to challenging healthcare questions. Partnerships between countries also aids in making global AI rules uniform. They can exchange information, and agree on the best way to implement those rules. All partners can benefit when they work together. These team projects make AI rules more trustworthy, and effective. They also support advancements, and growth. By studying successful projects, partners can use what they've learned in special situations. This helps them use AI in healthcare at its full potential.

While working together can be difficult, it's important. The trickiest part is managing everyone's different needs, and plans, which can possibly slow things down, and cause issues. Everyone needs to trust, and be open to, working together. This means speaking clearly, respecting one another, and aiming for the same goal. A team that trusts each other can handle difficulties, and achieve that goal together. Being open, and transparent, is just as vital as trust. Everyone must have the correct information to make smart choices. If all team members are honest, it builds belief, brings about responsibility, and sets up a space where everyone feels comfortable expressing their views. If teams face these issues head-on, they can use AI to improve healthcare exponentially, which in turn improves patient care.

7.3 Future-Proofing AI Policies: Adapting to Changes

AI is constantly changing, and this means our rules must also change. We must be ready for whatever changes come, and constantly plan for the "what ifs". This means considering potential issues in advance, testing different scenarios, and making strategies based on those scenarios. Creating policies that can keep up with fast-paced changes is challenging, but essential, especially in healthcare where AI can do many good things. These policies should be updated often, and flexible enough to be changed as needed. For instance, we could use a "sunset clause", meaning a policy won't last forever, unless we decide to keep it. In addition, policies should be periodically reviewed, and adjusted to match current events. By encouraging these changes, we ensure our AI rules can adapt, and improve as technology improves, making it even more helpful. This also fosters an adaptable environment where AI can flourish in healthcare, and realize its full potential.

AI rules are changing rapidly. With AI in so many places, we must consider how we use it. Policymakers must focus on making fair rules that cover problems like bias, privacy, and openness. They need to understand the ethical issues with AI, and make sure all AI systems are used safely, and wisely. Additionally, because AI is global, it's imperative we all play by the same rules. This helps everyone work together, globally, to create equal opportunities for AI growth. In this manner, people trust AI more, and know it's used to help everyone. Those in charge of AI also need to plan for the future, and constantly keep up with the latest AI innovations. By continually learning, they can ensure AI rules are doing their job, as well as protecting public healthcare.

Get ready for the future, laws should twist and turn, just like a dancer would in response to the changing beat. By putting future needs into the limelight, we can pave routes for policies that work for us, not against us. They should stick to the rhythm of every update, keeping an eye on all we might need to handle. This stage is what we need for AI to fit into healthcare safely, and effectively. Imagine better tools, and care built on a bottom line of responsibility. It improves, and aids health systems, sail the ever-changing seas of opportunity and challenge. Make a note: the ability to call, and answer to change, is the master key to making AI in healthcare work for us. In short, this part highlights the need to make policies for AI, so they're ready before we get to the chorus. The flexibility to change, and invent, ensures AI's safe, and thoughtful use. This approach is a win for the health sector, and also hits the target of making AI work for everyone. Next up, we'll delve into how AI impacts roles in healthcare, and how it's reshaping our relationships. It's a brave new world – let's see what it has in store for us!

8. Building Trust and Confidence in AI-Driven Solutions

I magine stepping into a hospital room, and a friendly AI buddy warmly explains your healthcare steps. This seems like it's from a futuristic movie, but it's actually happening now. The addition of artificial brains in healthcare is changing the game. This change could make patients' experiences better, and their care much smoother, but there's some concern. Many patients, and healthcare workers, are worried about AI's role. You might be asking, "Can I depend on this tech for my health"? We need to know how to ease these worries, which will help AI tools gain trust. This next part shares practical methods for calming patients, and clearly shows how AI is beneficial in the healthcare world.

8.1 Reassuring Patients: Communicating AI Benefits Effectively

Creating trust in AI is all about openness. Worries shrink when patients understand how AI works, and what its role is in their care. We must show them how they can benefit from AI, in layman's terms. Try describing AI as a tool that lets doctors spot health problems faster, and possibly before they occur. It might be helpful to have brochures detailing how AI helps get a diagnosis, and treatment plan, highlighting how it can be a huge benefit. Patient education programs are good ways to help patients connect with, and trust, AI. Think about setting up events like workshops that zoom in on AI and healthcare. These programs can take the mystery out of AI, showing patients what it can, and can't, do. Online study materials, and guides, can also be handy. They let patients dive deeper into AI on their own time, which helps them learn more, and erase any hesitations they may have. By putting many learning options on the table, we help patients make informed choices about their care. It's vital to include them on the AI journey, asking for their thoughts in feedback sessions, where they can air their views about using AI. These talks give us key insights into their feelings, allowing us to ease their minds, and emphasize how we will use AI. Engaging patient advisory boards in discussions about AI, is another smart move. When patients feel heard in the development, and roll-out, of AI technology, they'll understand how it works, and trust it more. This teamwork helps patients know they are a part of the process, know their concerns are valid, and will put their faith in AI-powered treatments.

Ensuring people using AI have their concerns, and questions answered, is key if we want them to trust it. We should have a handy list of answers available as to whether AI is safe, and what it can actually do. These answers should be easy to understand, based on facts, and help people feel at ease about how safe and reliable AI tools are. It can also be beneficial to have one-on-one meetings to talk with anyone who may still have reservations. In these meetings, healthcare workers can discuss how AI affects specific treatments, and care plans. This feels more personal, and helps each person feel listened to, and understood, making them comfortable with AI having a part in their healthcare experience.

8.2 Visual Element: Patient Engagement Infographic

Let's make an easy-to-understand picture that shows the best ways to make patients understand, and trust, AI. This picture, or infographic, should have parts like talking openly, teaching, listening to patients, and dealing with any concerns. Use small pictures, and graphs, to show how these methods help build trust. Healthcare workers can use this infographic as an aid, to help them use AI, and take care of their patients better. These methods can make them feel more secure, and be ready to rely on AI. Using these strategies, patients will see AI as a helpful tool in their healthcare journey.

8.3 Overcoming Skepticism: Case-Based Success Stories

In the healthcare field, there are many people who often question new technology. This includes AI, even if it will completely change how we care for patients. Still, several success stories are gradually altering the perception of AI. Consider this: AI can determine if a patient must return to the hospital, within a month after they're discharged, by looking at their data closely. This tech helps doctors, and nurses, act quickly to plan care that meets each patient's needs. As a result, the patient gets better, while the hospital saves money. AI can turn patient care from responding to an issue, to actively preventing it. There's also a fascinating way of using tech to help patients deal with long-term illnesses. Virtual health assistants, powered by AI, provide constant care to those patients. They can remind individuals to take their medicine, check their vitals, or follow their doctor's plan for staying healthy. These are crucial steps in treating illnesses like diabetes, or high blood pressure. Studies show AI assistants can improve patients' adherence to their treatment plans, by giving reminders, and instant feedback. These reminders, and custom treatment advice, from the AI, help patients stick to their treatment plans. They create a sense of duty in patients to take an active part in managing their health. This reduces the workload for healthcare professionals, and in the long run, improves how they care for their patients. AI's positive effects on healthcare can also be seen in medical imaging, as it helps decrease mistaken diagnoses. How, you ask? Analyzing medical images, with absolute precision, is often beyond human capability. AI technology can spot minute details that a person might miss, helping radiologists make more accurate diagnoses. This not only keeps patients safer, but also speeds up healthcare delivery, ultimately improving their overall health.

Professional healthcare workers share how AI helps them. Surgeons note that AI aids increase their precision, and speed, during surgery. Because of AI, they can use accurate data to make quick decisions, which can help patients recover faster, and avoid post-op problems. Nurses also talk about using AI to monitor their patients. AI that checks vital signals, and alerts them to any issues that arise, helps them act faster, which in turn, helps them to better care for their patients. These positive comments show how AI helps all healthcare workers, letting them spend more time caring for their patients, and less time doing paperwork. To address any possible doubts, we need to provide proof. Many researchers have confirmed the benefits of AI in healthcare, using comparison studies to prove that AI methods work better than the old ways, in many different areas. As an example, it has been found that AI is often more precise in finding specific health problems than traditional diagnosing methods. These studies confirm that AI can potentially improve healthcare services, and patients' recovery results. By showing this proof, healthcare providers can help patients, and their loved ones, feel more secure, and confident, in AI solutions.

8.4 Textual Element: Case Study Reflection

Remember in a previous chapter we discussed how AI is working well in doctors' offices, hospitals, and clinics? What makes it work? Have any problems arisen? Can it improve things if we use this case's know-how in our work? Think about how AI could change how we care for patients, helping doctors, and nurses, do their jobs better.

These thoughts should give you good ideas on how we are using AI in healthcare now, and how we can expect to use it moving forward. Looking at real-life examples, it's clear that AI isn't just a futuristic idea, it's something already being used to improve care for everyone.

8.5 Misdiagnoses and AI: Mitigating Risks Through Validation

AI can do amazing things in healthcare, but it's not without its hiccups. Diagnosing a disease incorrectly is a big concern, and can occur for many reasons, meaning there needs to be more variety in our training data. If all AI is programmed to use the same data, it might not be as accurate. This can lead to mistakes, especially when diagnosing diseases that manifest differently, in different people. A wide range of patient data needs to be collected to lower these risks. Mistakes can also happen when fine-tuning AI algorithms, as they need to be adjusted correctly, to work properly. If an algorithm is not programmed properly, it can generate the wrong results, leading to an incorrect diagnosis. To fix these problems, we need to be very careful when developing, and testing, AI systems. For protection against these risks, we need strong rules, and must put AI systems through strict tests that mimic real-world situations, before they're installed. This helps us locate, and fix, any issues that may arise. It is also important to closely monitor how the AI systems perform. Health workers can ensure they remain accurate, and effective, by regularly performing quality checks. In this way, they can step in, and institute any needed changes, making AI more reliable in the healthcare field.

Using safety measures in AI-assisted health checks can reduce the chances of a wrong diagnosis, and people are the key. Even though AI can sort data faster, and more precisely, it is not meant to work alone. When you include healthcare experts in these check-up processes, you ensure experienced people are monitoring AI-generated results. This teamwork approach makes the most of human insight, and computer exactness, increasing the accuracy of diagnoses. In addition, backup systems, and manual checks, provide extra safety measures, spotting mistakes before any harm can be done. This maximizes AI gains, while minimizing any related risks.

In image-based medicine, AI systems work successfully with humans. X-ray specialists work with AI tools, to examine their findings, and confirm diagnoses. This cooperation increases accuracy, and builds faith in AI. Another suitable method is setting up AI mistakes reporting. These systems let healthcare providers document, and study, AI mistakes, revealing problem areas to improve. By focusing on the errors' root causes, healthcare groups can fine-tune their AI, and reduce future wrong diagnoses. These instances stress the need for a bold approach to lowering risk, and show how well-planned AI use can make healthcare delivery safer, and more reliable.

Textual Element: Risk Mitigation Checklist

Double-check these steps to make sure your AI systems work right:

1. Make sure your training data includes a variety of patients.
2. Test your AI systems well.
3. Always check how your AI works in real-world doctors' offices.
4. Have doctors participate in the AI diagnosis process.
5. Set up backup systems, and perform checks by hand, to double-check how AI does.
6. Have a system for reporting mistakes by AI, and a plan to fix them.

Here's a simple guide for healthcare groups. It helps to build a strong plan to lower the dangers of using AI for diagnoses. The aim is to make patient care safer, and work better.

8.6 AI as a Healthcare Partner: Stories from the Field

AI is like a new friend in the changing world of healthcare. It changes how medical people plan, do, and look at medical actions. Think about how we prepare for surgery. AI systems analyze data from past surgeries, and patient histories, which helps make operations safer, and more accurate, allowing doctors to see problems before they happen. This is an excellent example of how people, and AI, can work together to improve surgery. Medical professionals use AI to look at patient data, making it easier to create care plans that are tailored for each patient. Doctors can make suggestions based on data, by using AI's innovative abilities, which promotes trust, and communication between patient, and provider. This approach makes care personal, and motivates patients to get involved.

AI is moving healthcare in new directions. For one, it makes emergency care faster, and more efficient. By looking at essential patient details, AI can quickly determine the order in which patients are seen. Cutting down wait times, and using medical supplies better, can save lives. In addition, AI can assist with virtual medical care, meaning patients can get professional advice, without having to visit a clinic. With extra help from AI tools, these chats let doctors assess patients from a distance, which can help bring good-quality healthcare to more people. Using AI in healthcare isn't always easy, however, people have shared positive stories, giving us valuable tips. As an example, nurses appreciate AI's ability to monitor their patients, because they can't be in every room at the same time. It can keep track of a patient's vital signs, and warn the medical team of any issues, which allows for quicker response times. Doctors also find that with info from AI, they can fine-tune diagnoses, and treatment plans.

Another way AI can assist in the healthcare field is by reducing paperwork for staff. Its systems can handle tasks like scheduling, billing, and record keeping, leaving healthcare staff more time for patient care. The change from paperwork, to patient care, increases job satisfaction, and enriches the patient experience. In addition, AI tools improve the quality of virtual appointments between patients, and providers. By using them for these chats, healthcare providers ensure patients are up-to-date with their care, and treatment plans. This elevated level of communication promotes a feeling of teamwork, and reliance, which is essential for good healthcare. When we think about the different applications, and benefits, of AI in healthcare, it's clear that this tech is more than just a machine; it's a partner in improving care for everyone.

From pre-op, to patient check-ins, AI helps healthcare professionals provide better, more customized care. By reducing paperwork, and improving virtual medicine, AI allows providers to focus on the most essential thing – caring for their patients. Moving to the next chapter, we will delve into how AI's combination shapes healthcare methods, and patient results.

9. Collaborative Approaches to AI Implementation

In today's bustling hospitals, teamwork isn't just a word, it's essential, especially when using AI. I remember when a young doctor was stumped by an intricate new AI tool used for diagnoses. A meeting with the tech expert who created the system explained how to use it. This conversation kicked off a joint effort that improved the tool's use. It showed me how powerful it can be when health workers, and tech people, work together. This type of team effort helps us get the most out of AI, letting us provide better care to our patients, while making hospital tasks more efficient. When they work together, with mutual respect, common goals are achieved, with each bringing unique knowledge to the table, that opens the door to new ideas. Healthcare workers provide an understanding of patient care, daily procedures, and medical practice subtleties. Tech experts offer their knowledge of AI, software creation, and tying systems together. When these viewpoints combine, it results in better problem-solving. Different expertise lets teams view issues from various sides, leading to stronger, more valuable solutions. For example, when an AI tool for diagnoses is being made, healthcare professionals can point out clinical needs, while tech experts focus on the technical aspect of the solutions. Working together fills gaps in knowledge, ensuring innovative AI applications are practical, and user-friendly.

Healthcare, and tech, are teaming up, and making a big splash. Think about it - they're creating AI tools that allow for early detection of diseases. In the same way, joint research is leading to new AI treatments, developed for each person's unique needs. They do this by combining clinical know-how, with top-level tech, showing that working together can make a real difference, by pushing medical science forward. Communication is key in any successful venture, so to smoothly introduce AI tech, teams need that communication to be clear. Tools like project software, and video chats, can give updates in real-time, helping teams stay in touch, no matter where they are, and make sure everyone's on the same page. Regular meetings amongst different fields, are also important. They provide opportunities to discuss progress, and obstacles, in order to provide support, and solutions. By keeping the lines of communication open, teams can handle the challenges of AI rollout more quickly, and efficiently. Even so, working together can be challenging at times. Different teams may have other goals, which can lead to tension. Healthcare workers might prioritize patient outcomes, and safety, while tech teams look at innovation, and system performance. Clearly stating project goals, ensuring everyone understands, and agrees, is key. This helps unify the team, driving them towards the same outcome. Building mutual respect, and understanding each teams' role in the process, can help bridge any gaps between them. This ensures that all ideas are valued, and considered, when making decisions.

Textual Element: Handy Tips to Talk

- Embrace Team Tools: Stay current with task-tracking software and video calls in your project management.
- Plan Routine Gatherings: Set up meetings every week with all fields included. Here, we discuss advances, problems, and ways to solve them.

- Set Goals Clearly: Make sure the team goals are agreeable, and attainable.
- Boost Shared Respect: Open conversations help a lot. All ideas, no matter how varied, add value to our teamwork.

So, what's the final word? When tech wizards, and healthcare professionals, team up, huge progress can be made. If we play nice together, we can make the most out of AI in the healthcare environment. This also encourages new ideas, and research, making strides to improve patient care. When teams have disagreements, open communication, and compromise, are keys to finding the best solutions to the issues. Preparing for a future where AI can streamline the healthcare field is pretty cool, right?

9.1 Building Interdisciplinary AI Teams: Best Practices

Forming an AI team that works well together. requires choosing people with different skills, and know-how. You'll need to find data whizzes, and AI experts, who can develop, and utilize, fancy algorithms. This team knows the ins and outs of AI, from machine learning to deep learning, and can provide data that makes sense. Doctors, and other healthcare workers, also part of the team, bring their invaluable knowledge, and experience, to the table. They know exactly what their patients need, and how medical protocols work, making sure AI ideas are innovative, and practical. By merging tech, and healthcare skills, the team can produce solutions that improve healthcare for everyone. Because the expertise of each team member is varied, their combined minds can look at problems from every angle, ensuring their solutions are accurate, and valuable. Weekly scheduled meetings, where everyone shares ideas, is a key component in accomplishing this goal. They foster creativity, and lay the groundwork, for new ways of thinking. Projects run more efficiently when the team is focused on end game, aligning tasks with the bigger picture. Flexible plans allow them to change, and adapt quickly, to new developments. This engaging setup enables each member to use their unique ability, and skill set, to make the project stronger as a whole.

Project leaders play a crucial role in this process, overseeing each team, and ensuring mutual cooperation. These leaders encourage their crew members, and create all-inclusive environments, where every persons' opinions are heard. In an atmosphere of shared trust, and respect, leaders promote candid conversation, and cooperation. These settings let members put forth their ideas, without fear, knowing their contributions are valued. Another advantage to having a team leader includes outlining the objectives, and delegating responsibilities, making certain everyone is clear on what their duties are. Those in leadership empower members to focus on their strengths, and collaborate effectively, while continuously providing support. A robust leader directs the team's efforts, promotes a sense of cohesion, and commitment, setting the team up for success.

There are critical practices for building, and maintaining, effective interdisciplinary AI teams. Structuring clear objectives and roles, from the start, lays a solid foundation for teamwork. Well-defined objectives help align the team's efforts, making sure that everyone is working towards the same purpose. Continual development in professional skills is another core driver of team success. Team members can stay ahead of the curve, in AI development, by encouraging each other to never stop learning. This dedication to learning cultivates an environment that breeds innovation, and adaptability, paving the way for teams to grow in the fast-paced world of AI tech. By putting these best practices into action, teams can increase their effectiveness, therefore pushing the boundaries of their ability to deliver profound AI solutions in healthcare.

Interactive Element: Team Dynamics Reflection

Take a moment to think about your team's makeup. Each person brings unique skills and knowledge. Are there gaps where added skills could boost your team's power? In addition, think about how you work together. Do you often join forces in group workshop sessions, or idea-sharing meetings? Look at your team's leaders, too. Do they cultivate a work environment that includes, and inspires, everyone? Put some thought into how you could improve the way you all work as a cohesive unit, utilizing the tips highlighted in this section.

9.2 Cross-Sector Innovation: Healthcare Meets Technology

Healthcare and tech are shaking hands, opening up a whole new world of fresh ideas. They're using AI to help doctors better communicate with their patients, and build custom-made health plans. AI can correlate, and summarize, patient information faster, all while anticipating a patient's health needs. This allows doctors to recognize health concerns earlier, and provide care sooner. It's a seismic shift from waiting for something to happen, to stopping that something before it even starts. The Internet of Things, or IoT, makes this work even more effectively. It connects healthcare gadgets, and systems, that monitor and care for patients. Imagine a world where your smartwatch talks to your doctor, and delivers real-time data back to you, which helps you make an informed decision about your care. It would mark a significant step forward, making healthcare quicker, and more efficient.

Take a look at some of the cool stuff that happens when healthcare, and technology, team up. A perfect example is telehealth services that use AI. Thanks to them, people living in remote, or hard-to-reach places, can still get excellent healthcare. AI can discover patients' needs, schedule appointments, and provide care through video meetings. This means more people have access to healthcare, and the quality of that care remains top-notch. Another exciting project is the creation of super-smart hospitals that use AI and IoT. In these groundbreaking hospitals, AI manages everything from how patients move around the hospital, to how energy is used. This results in better patient care, fewer resources used, and a healthcare environment that can change, and adapt as needed.

Innovation in different areas can lead to outstanding new projects, where specific policies are key. These policies make room for trying new things, and bringing fresh tech onboard. Grants, sponsored by the government for AI research, make it possible for innovators to develop new technology. They can blaze a new trail, without worrying about funding, which stimulates creativity. Partnerships between the public, and private sectors, also boost innovation by sharing resources, and know-how. Such teamwork forms a nurturing environment, leading to creative, and practical ideas. Even so, innovation across sectors can face significant hurdles. We must work around those to keep pushing forward, and make a real difference.

Rules can often present unique challenges. Adopting new tech may be hindered by complex, and sometimes antiquated, regulations. To move beyond them, innovators, and regulators, must join hands, and work together. Collaboration will ensure safety remains the primary concern, while they can, simultaneously, lobby for new laws that will include today's healthcare realities. Others may have reservations, causing conflicts that can halt innovation. Being transparent, finding new avenues of communication, and encouraging education, are a few ways we can use to overcome any objections. Providing every necessary, and available, tool to all healthcare professionals, allows them to care for their patients in the best way possible, and that is the ultimate goal,

9.3 Learning from Other Industries: AI Integration Insights

AI isn't just used in healthcare; many other fields continuously improve, and innovate, tech. Take finance, for example, where AI helps with risk analysis, and detecting fraud. Banks, and finance companies, use AI to spot fraudulent patterns in millions of transactions a day. Belief in the security of their systems is imperative, and they rely on this tech to maintain it. This is also true in medicine, where AI can improve the way data is stored, keeping patients' personal information confidential. It can also detect any breaches in security, immediately, which can prevent possible damage from data leakage. In the retail world, they've become pros at crafting individual customer experiences. Using AI to gather, and analyze consumer data, they're able to predict the shopping habits of their consumers. We, as healthcare providers, can also use this method to develop patient care plans that are more specific, and customized for each individual patient. Picture a world where AI looks at a patient's medical records, and lifestyle habits, then produces personalized health advice. It would include diet recommendations, fitness plans, a medication schedule, and any other information the patient may require. This could be ideal for preventive care, and patient engagement, getting them more involved in the process. By implementing retail strategies, i.e. being customer focused, healthcare professionals provide faster, better, and more personalized care that builds stronger patient relationships.

Integrating AI into healthcare requires careful planning. Agile methods, popular in tech circles for quick timing tests, greatly help health-related AI tasks. Agile is about making changes step-by-step, letting teams quickly adjust to remarks, and changing needs. Adaptability is a must in healthcare! The patients' needs, and tech's skills, are constantly updating. Using agile methods, healthcare teams can create new AI tools that reflect real-life needs. Similarly, making choices based on data, the norm in tech and finance, is also handy in healthcare. The data helps medical experts make choices that improve patient health, and using data analysis makes things run smoother. We can see this in supply chain improvement, as an example, wherein methods are borrowed from shipping services, and utilized in healthcare. With AI models predicting, and handling supply needs, healthcare facilities can ensure necessary supplies are always at the ready, meaning less waste, and better resource handling. It has helped hospitals run more efficiently, and save money. Another instance is patient contact programs that take cues from selling strategies. AI-supported data analysis can identify patients who are more likely to miss an appointment, or not follow their treatment plans, allowing healthcare providers to intervene ahead of time.

Although AI can be useful, it's not an easy task to utilize it in the healthcare realm. What we learn about the use of AI from other fields, will help shape its usage in healthcare moving forward. While AI can be a valuable resource, it is essential to consider the patients, and their needs. Accordingly, we need to find the perfect balance between using new technology, and communicating with our patients. There are also laws in the healthcare world that need to be considered. Unlike some fields, healthcare has regulations designed to keep patients' personal information completely secure, and confidential. At times, these rules can make it more difficult to implement new technology like AI, which indicates the need for careful planning, to work within the parameters of them. Acting jointly with the governing bodies that set forth these rules, and taking the needs of each patient into consideration, healthcare providers can employ AI in a way that is not only innovative, but also within the guidelines.

10. Preparing for the Future of Healthcare AI

I n the fast-moving tech world, healthcare is at a thrilling crossroad of innovative, and amazing, possibilities. Think of a young scientist at a busy conference. She listens, in awe, to a lecture on how AI is changing healthcare, today, not in some far-off future. Events like these, underline how crucial preparing for AI in the healthcare world is. As we dive into this adventure, let's explore AI's trends, and possibilities, that will help you stay ahead. AI advancements are reshaping healthcare, offering excellent new options in technology. The way AI, and genomics, are working together, is an exciting example. They use a patient's unique DNA to design the best possible treatments, and care plans. AI can also use this information to predict how a patient may react to their medications, making it easier for doctors to prescribe what's safest.

The use of AI in special augmented reality glasses, is changing how doctors and nurses treat their patients. Picture medical school students using these glasses to see additional details on the human body, as they learn. These AI advancements greatly affect the speed in which patients can receive diagnoses, and treatments, effectively improving how the healthcare system works. It also allows patients to actively participate in their own healthcare journey, making them feel included, which in turn, inspires them to follow their doctor's instructions.

AI is transforming our world, and one of the exciting new ideas is to create a machine for in-home health checkups. The device will allow people to keep track of their health, from the comfort of their living room, using AI-powered software. The software can analyze the collected data, then give custom health advice, or tell the person if they need to see the doctor. This can be especially helpful for people with chronic health issues, making healthcare more accessible, and comfortable. AI can also assist with making healthcare accessible to everyone. It can spot where, and why, some people have trouble getting care, and design unique programs to overcome these deficits. This will ensure everyone has access to fair, and equal, healthcare.

Interactive Component: Network Interaction Guide for AI Enthusiasts

- Find and join professional groups that focus on AI.
- Attend online seminars, meetings, and training events for new ideas, and networking.
- Talk about, and share, your own experiences in AI with colleagues to add to our common understanding.
- Consistently read updates from trade magazines, professional articles, and blogs, to keep in touch with the newest changes in AI.

10.1 Continuous Learning: Professional Development in AI

In the ever-changing world of healthcare, continuing education is vital. Because of AI advancements, healthcare professionals must develop new skills, and know-how. Becoming accustomed to new AI tools can be a challenge that requires a dedicated commitment to learning. Fortunately, there are workshops and conferences healthcare workers can attend to gain a better understanding of AI, and what role it will play in the future. These events provide them the opportunity to learn from AI experts, and join focus groups with their peers. Online classes, and certifications, are also beneficial to continued education. These classes dig into the different aspects of AI, with levels from beginner to expert, offering flexible learning options, and timetables, to fit any individual's schedule.

Hospitals play an important role, acting as a place for non-stop learning, and creativity. By helping their staff grow, these hospitals have become a center of fresh ideas that keep pace with changes. One brilliant idea is having AI teaching centers onsite that become hotspots for learning, giving staff access to resources, and the newest tech. In addition, if staff take AI learning courses independently, the hospitals can offer tuition reimbursement. By offering this perk, workers will be motivated to continue learning, and it shows the hospitals are dedicated to furthering their employees' education. Putting money into these programs, hospitals inspire their workforce to get more comfortable using AI technologies. Hospitals can partner with colleges and universities, resulting in access to top-notch classes, and professors. These partnerships allow hospitals to create an active learning environment that ensures their staff have everything they need to implement AI into their daily routines. It's an important factor to balance continuing education, and growth, in a field that changes rapidly. As AI technologies advance, the skills and knowledge of healthcare professionals must also advance. By accepting educational resources and training, healthcare organizations can be places for developing fresh ideas. As a result, better quality care is provided to their patients.

If you're a healthcare professional, being well informed of AI's potential, and growth, is vitally important. Joining AI focus groups can offer valuable opportunities to learn more about this new, and exciting, technology. These groups recruit specialists from various fields, who share their knowledge, and discuss the development of fresh ideas. Reading industry magazines, and articles, can also be beneficial, as they offer the latest research, case studies, and experts' opinions, in regard to AI in healthcare. Continuing education can make you a valuable asset, providing excellent opportunities for the advancement of your career,

10.2 Future Scenarios: AI's Role in Healthcare Evolution

Picture this: you step into a health center, and are greeted by intelligent machines - from welcoming you to the office and checking you in, all the way to assisting in surgery, robots lend a hand, working with perfect accuracy. AI software constantly monitors your health, discovers any issues, and can prevent them from becoming more severe. Far from being a science-fiction movie, this could soon be a reality, thanks to rapidly advancing AI tech. This progression in healthcare isn't just about doing things faster; it's about creating a better patient experience, and providing better care. AI is helping to individualize health systems, shaping every patient's journey to their specific needs. In turn, patients get a more significant say in their healthcare decisions, and better results. AI is changing more than just how things are done in the clinic; it's also completely reshaping the health sector. More and more people are employing virtual care, and "telehealth", with the help of AI, which allows for round-the-clock care, and advice. Patients can talk to healthcare professionals without leaving their homes, getting help exactly when they need it, making healthcare more accessible. Utilizing these options also alleviates pressure off healthcare facilities by, reducing traffic. Another way AI is shaking up the healthcare world is the way medications are prescribed. It can analyze heaps of data to determine what works best for each individual, fine-tune treatment plans, and limit "trial-and-error" methods. This targeted approach lowers costs, and leaves patients feeling more confident.

Ethics play a key role with regard to health systems run by AI. Its decisions must be clear, and concise, to maintain trust and fairness in patient care. There are also questions about who is liable if an AI system makes a mistake. Finding the answers will mean setting new rules, in a combined effort, with tech experts, ethicists, medical professionals, and lawmakers. While AI can reap enormous benefits for personal, and proactive patient care, the guidelines for its use must be concrete. With its ability to predict future issues, healthcare professionals can stay ahead of the game when it comes to patients' needs. The ability to step in quickly can prevent future health issues, and improve results. This forward-looking model moves us from merely reacting to an existing health problem, to keeping people healthy in the first place.

Healthcare organizations, and teams, must be forward thinking, and flexible about what's coming. Using planning tools, and activities, help them do that, and respond to future changes. Through planning, they discover potential problems, and opportunities for growth. It's also essential to have flexible, and scalable technology systems at the ready. As AI grows, healthcare systems need to be able to implement new tools, and features, quickly. By investing in adaptable technology systems, organizations can improve AI without requiring significant updates. Additionally, this aids them in working smoothly, and more efficiently. Healthcare workers play an essential part in driving AI use, and creating new ways to utilize it. They need to constantly look for ways to improve, and work together to change how healthcare is provided. By working with assorted teams, and staying current on AI developments, these groups can spot new trends, and tackle whatever may come. As AI keeps shaping healthcare's future, the ability to adapt, and innovate, will be the key to better patient care, and enduring success.

10.3 Preparing for Disruption: Embracing Change

Healthcare is undergoing significant changes. The rapid development of AI is reshaping everything, testing age-old roles, and routines. In a hospital where AI attends to patient check-ins, healthcare experts are afforded more time to focus on treatment, as opposed to clerical duties. This is not about machines replacing human interaction, as nurses, and doctors, would be more readily available to treat their patients, making decisions with information backed up by AI insights. By asking for a change in mindset, and welcoming new methods, AI should be seen as a friend, and not a threat to the heart of healthcare. Technological changes are influencing how patients are cared for, and managed. AI tools transform how we diagnose, plan treatments, and follow-up with patients. They can study patient data, and spot potential health issues, before any symptoms appear, changing the outcome in a positive way. These new methods require healthcare professionals to think differently, so bringing technology to the table, in ways unimageable before, becomes the norm. This disruption in routine requires fresh perspective, ensuring technology supports human knowledge, rather than outdoing it.

Adapting to change well, doctors, and other healthcare workers, need to be open to new ideas. Trying new things, and tweaking them to make them better, even a little at a time, is very important. Smoothly handling change is possible when we incorporate new technology, while also improving that technology, based on what we learn from it. When staff feels like they are part of the process, patient care improves. If we believe we can continually learn, and grow, we are open to new ideas, and will seek out the answers we need for success. This way of thinking changes a problem into a solution, which brings new ideas, and steady progress. For health professionals, being informed, and ready to incorporate the use of new tools as they become available, is vital.

Leaders who are ready to adjust to change themselves, are best at guiding their teams through the complex task of using AI. They lead by example, embracing the changes that, ultimately, help us reach our goal of incorporating AI into the healthcare professions. Great leaders encourage teams to trust each other, and make their staff feel valued. This ability increases morale, job satisfaction, and gets everyone excited about the changes to come. Leaders who talk openly, and honestly, build strong teams that are ready to embrace every change AI brings.

With AI included in their daily routines, hospitals, doctors' offices, and clinics, can diagnose illnesses faster, and more accurately. Collectively, these facilities use AI to share health records with each other, ensuring patients receive consistent care, no matter where they're being treated. Looking at the future of healthcare, the AI road ahead is full of opportunities. It's becoming clear that adapting to these new technologies is imperative. Learning to embrace these changes lets us tap into all that AI can offer, thus making the medical field more efficient, improving patient care exponentially.

11. Visualizing the Future: AI's Long-term Impact

I magine a busy health clinic, hidden away in a distant village. The nurse in charge uses a modern tablet, powered by AI, to check each patient's health. While this may sound like science fiction, it's happening today, worldwide. The influence of AI in healthcare is growing, bringing many exciting changes, but also some tough challenges. AI could make a huge difference in places where health resources are scarce. For example, new online healthcare platforms are changing how people in isolated areas receive care, connecting patients with experts, no matter how far apart they are. Ensuring people in rural communities receive the care they need, in a timely manner, is greatly beneficial, but there's a catch. The use of AI may differ from one area to another, so cultural factors need to be taken into consideration. In some areas, patients may be wary of new technology, needing clearcut information, and education, to help them understand AI, and learn to trust it.

Different parts of the world share their own AI success stories in healthcare. In Africa, AI is a lifeline. People who live in remote areas can now consult doctors, and receive treatment plans, without traveling far. AI solutions are being personalized to fight common diseases like malaria, and tuberculosis. These diseases are widespread in certain areas, but AI can help, by predicting when, and where, the next outbreak may occur, and tells us how to best use our resources. This shows how AI can be adjusted to work in different regions, making healthcare systems function better, and improving overall health. There are still big differences in the use of AI between first and third world nations. We must plan, and initiate steps, to share technology, building a network that can cross every socioeconomic line. International partnerships can promote this sharing of knowledge, but more importantly, resources. In this way, we can guarantee that the use of AI in healthcare, is beneficial in every corner of the world.

Collaboration between countries is an important component to improving AI in the healthcare field, promoting worldwide learning, and teamwork. The World Health Organization, (WHO), played an important role in launching programs like the Global Initiative on AI for Health. This particular program unites experts from different sectors, who collectively set ethical rules, and governing plans, for using AI in healthcare. Partnerships for research, beyond borders, show how powerful working together can be. These relationships accelerate AI development by merging resources, and knowledge, that can discover breakthroughs in technology, which one group alone could not. As an example, working in concert on AI applications that research rare diseases, has led to significant developments that offer hope to patients all over the world. Highlighting the importance of working together on AI development, shows how we can fully use its power to change healthcare worldwide.

11.1 AI-Driven Healthcare Ecosystems: A Vision for Integration

A healthcare system, powered by AI, is like magic. Consider a hospital that uses AI for everything: welcoming patients; intake forms; managing resources; inventory; appointment, surgery, and staff scheduling, all in the same system. Within this same network, patients' health records are also stored securely. These records can be instantly updated by the doctors, and nurses, who treat these patients, and AI can collate the data looking for any patterns. Having this information at their fingertips, healthcare professionals can save countless hours spent doing paperwork, allowing them to spend more time caring for their patients. Patients can also have access to their health records through the use of AI-powered apps, any time, day or night. They can monitor their health, book appointments, and communicate with their doctors. These tools help patients be healthier, feel more in control of their health journey, and can lower the cost of their healthcare.

Using AI in healthcare may sound complicated, but in actuality, it simplifies things! It helps doctors, and nurses, communicate more effectively, and aids them in making the best decisions for their patients. AI uses up-to-the-minute data to give doctors quick, and competent, information. In this manner, doctors can make on the spot diagnoses, saving their patients from a long, drawn out, process. Additionally, AI can manage where equipment should be located, and when, as well as maintain all the systems in the facility itself. Some of the smartest hospitals, that have already implemented AI, are getting good results. They can manage things like how a patient "moves" through the hospital; from exam room, to surgery, to recovery, to the room they'll stay in until they're well enough to go home. AI can also run tests on the hospital's equipment, and arrange for its repair, when necessary.

11.2 Advocacy and Community Building: Shaping AI's Future

Helping others is key in directing the path of AI use in healthcare. By protecting patient rights, medical professionals ensure AI is used ethically, and morally. Groups that advocate for patients' rights, work tirelessly for fair AI rules, ensuring that personal data is secure, while using these powerful tools. They stress that healthcare companies must be transparent about their use of AI, respecting their patients' feelings, and privacy. These rules also stress the need for the creation of AI programs that adapt, for all kinds of people, understanding that different ethnic groups, all have different healthcare needs. It's also important to understand that doing the right thing should always come before developing new tech, just for the sake of it.

Building a sense of community is essential when working together, making it easier to share knowledge. Networks of healthcare professionals, focused on AI, create places where experts can swap information, and collaborate on new ideas. These experts can, collectively, develop new AI projects that would be hard to do alone. Shared research projects are an essential part of consolidating information, and accelerating the process of developing new AI tools that are exciting, useful, and practical.

Many groups are working to ensure the integrity of AI is maintained in the healthcare fields. The diversity of these groups, from those who make the rules to those who look after our health, ensure that AI helps meet public health standards. Being clear, and concise, about what needs to be done, is essential. By involving people from different communities, and knowing more about AI's power, we can work towards this goal. Partnering with institutes of learning, and further research, helps create evidence-based policies, and practices, building a continually improving healthcare culture.

11.3 Empowering Innovation: Lessons from AI Pioneers

Innovators don't sit around waiting for AI improvements to magically appear. They roll up their sleeves, and dive headfirst into researching, and discovering, new ways to make healthcare better. Looking at the AI-guided tools they've already developed, for diagnosing diseases, has changed how we view healthcare, making it a faster, and more accurate, process. Building tailored AI for healthcare has pushed the boundaries, creating treatments centered around each persons' genes, meaning the door has opened to new health solutions that match our individual complexities. These inventors work around the clock, creating new AI tools that will eventually help patients recover more quickly, giving them a better healthcare experience. These AI change-makers have a blend of traits, and methods, that make them different. They think ahead, and spot opportunities where most people see problems, building ethical AI technologies that are both handy, and responsible. Understanding the magic of research, innovators develop partnerships across various fields. This teamwork creates a unique space where new thoughts can grow, and develop, to make giant leaps in the healthcare world that impact everyone.

Here's what we can learn from these leaders who are the first to use new techniques successfully. They often face strict guidelines, and regulations, but don't let that stop them. Instead, they use their imaginations, and never give up, working with rule-makers to ensure they're doing what's right, while pushing for changes that support trying new things. One key lesson they teach us, is creating solutions using new technologies that can grow, and change over time, without causing harm. These pioneers think about how to make their developments work in different situations, while also reaching as many people as possible, creating a path for those hoping to follow in their footsteps. By sharing their personal stories, developers offer a peek into the hard work, and excitement, needed to make fundamental changes in healthcare utilizing new technologies. These stories provide rare insights into their challenges, and victories, that can spark creativity in those aspiring to contribute to the field of AI. Welcoming change can reimagine healthcare, and pave the way for a future where new technology improves patient care.

11.4 Bridging the Digital Divide: Ensuring Inclusive AI Access

The lack of access to AI technology presents many hurdles, especially in healthcare. As an example, the elderly are not as comfortable doing everything online, or remotely. Others may live in rural areas where internet is not available, and don't have the money for fancy equipment. Many people. who need help the most, don't have proper digital systems in place. These factors make it even more difficult for them to

102 AI In Healthcare

use AI for their health needs. Bridging these gaps, so everyone can benefit from AI, will require some innovative thinking. Erecting cell towers, and better digital systems, to increase coverage in areas where they're most needed, is a great start. This includes the expansion of internet, and mobile services, for people who are currently out of range, but also making it more affordable, can definitely help. With fair pricing, and wallet-friendly tools, better healthcare won't just be reserved for those with more money. By implementing these strategies, we can level the AI playing field, making quality healthcare accessible for many more people.

Many programs have already been created to help people gain fair access to AI. Local tech education classes offer the training, and the tools, to give people the skills they need to become more familiar with the use of AI. These classes also get people excited about how AI can improve the quality of their healthcare services. Mobile health centers, with AI tools, are a great way to bring healthcare to the communities needing them most, that they may not otherwise have access to. This shows how targeted programs can fill in the gaps, and allow more people to have access to tech advances. While a lot of headway has already been made, there's still more work to be done to give everyone an equal chance at benefitting from the digital world. Governments, NGOs, and businesses, need to come together to build new infrastructure, and roll out programs that provide these services to people, at a reasonable cost. Their joint efforts can gather the resources, and the know-how, to accelerate the growth of new digital networks. People in the communities these programs benefit can also take part in crafting, and implementing, these solutions. This ensures that AI tech is fine-tuned to meet local needs, ultimately improving an individual's access to healthcare.

11.5 Transformative Case Studies: AI's Impact Across Borders

AI has played, and continues to play, a significant role in some of the biggest worldwide health issues, most notably during the COVID-19 pandemic. It can assimilate tons of information instantly, providing answers that make sense. This gave healthcare professionals essential insights that helped slow the spread of the virus. Using AI for contact tracing, predicting where it would spread, became key in dealing with this public health crisis. In countries like South Korea, AI was used to track the virus, and predict where it might go next, making it possible to provide aid much faster, in places it was most needed. Partnerships, across world borders, have also led to some significant findings in AI technology. Researchers around the world have worked together, using AI to identify rare disease markers in our DNA. This joint effort has made it faster to find new treatments, bringing hope to those with limited choices.

In order for these projects to shine, great leaders, and planning, were extremely important. These leaders, who believed in AI's power, integrated AI into existing health programs, making a place that welcomed new ideas. Collaboration between different cultures called for clear-cut conversations. With language barriers, and different rules, there were a few hurdles to overcome. Navigating through the diverse legalities of each region was required, and a profound grasp of local laws was necessary. Forming multi-cultural teams, and working with local law-makers from the start, built trust, and ensured all issues were addressed. Global teamwork, and broad-mindedness, made it possible for AI to work successfully.

Two essential factors are needed for AI's continued success. It needs to grow, and adapt to new technology as it comes along. The tools will need to be tailored to each place it is utilized, and as it grows, stronger systems will need to be developed. Integrating new technology into these systems will also require teams to support, and maintain, them. These teams can share information, and know-how, while cooperating with research facilities, and medical professionals. Having strong ties with government regulators will be imperative, as well, to move AI's new advances forward, allowing it to improve healthcare around the world.

11.6 The Role of AI in Achieving Healthcare Equality

Good healthcare is something everyone should have access to, no matter who they are, or where they come from. However, for some people it may be more difficult to get the care they need. That's where AI comes in! Providing health services to people who often go unnoticed, is a hole AI can fill, finding new ways to reach those in need. How, you ask? Well, let's look at some elements that can impact our health. Other than the usual culprits like diet, and exercise, the kind of house we live in, our education, how much money we earn, and environmental conditions, are also important factors that affect how healthy we are. AI tools can collate this information, and predict which communities might be more likely to suffer from a lack of quality health services. Using this knowledge, AI can help bring fair health treatment to everyone!

Equality in healthcare can be a challenging goal to attain. This is often because resources aren't fairly distributed, meaning some communities are left out, and receive fewer benefits. One reason for this is AI can sometimes be biased, which happens when the data it learns from, only represents some people, and not all, producing unfair results. AI can help resolve this bias with information gleaned from areas not previously included. Teaming up with the people inside these overlooked communities, gathering their health histories, and lifestyle choices, gives AI a broader spectrum to work with. Analyzing this new data will produce more accurate results, making it possible to redistribute those resources accordingly. In turn, healthcare providers now have the tools they need, exactly where they need them, ensuring the same quality of care is equally provided to everyone.

11.7 Looking Forward: AI's Promise for Future Generations

AI will play a significant role in tomorrow's healthcare world, leading to new ways of making people healthier, and their lives better. Already, AI is being used in medicine to solve complex health problems; its talent for handling massive amounts of data, enables us to discover new medicines, and treatments, faster than ever before. AI is also about understanding illnesses better, not just finding new ways to treat them. Think of a world where AI constantly monitors our health; creating daily plans for each individual, based on their unique genetic make-up, and lifestyle. This not only helps in discovering health problems earlier, but lets people participate in making decisions about their own care; helping them live longer, healthier lives. AI innovation can mean a future where illnesses are predicted, and prevented, not just treated after they've already been diagnosed.

The longevity of AI is essential, so our grandchildren, and their grandchildren, can reap its benefits. It needs a lot of power, so we also need to be eco-friendly, keeping AI's carbon footprint small. Being ethical in how we grow, and use AI, is just as important. Its systems must remain completely secure, respecting privacy, but also be open about how they operate, which are keys in building trust. Ensuring that AI works for all communities is also crucial; eliminating bias by inputting data from all ethnicities, and cultures. Responsibly focusing on inclusion, we develop AI that respects our values, while also improving our quality of life.

Getting young people interested in, and excited about AI development, sets us up for what lies ahead. Teaching kids about AI gives them the knowledge they need, not only to make significant improvements in existing technology, but also develop new ideas that can be implemented in the future. Collaboration within a diverse group makes everyone feel heard, and can result in many creative solutions. When they think about the possibilities of AI, it allows them to tackle the complex problems we might face moving forward. As the future inventors, and leaders of the AI revolution, these young people will be using it to make a difference, helping people all over the world stay healthy.

Conclusion

We've come far in exploring how AI is changing healthcare. This book shows just how much it affects, and will continue to affect, patient care, diagnostics, and health systems, around the world. Looking at a wide range of new ideas, and possibilities of how virtual health assistants will help patients with diagnoses, and treatments, we can see how beneficial using AI-driven predictions will be. We've tried to make complex ideas easy for medical professionals, creative minds, and patients. Explaining how machine learning, and deep learning, change how we diagnose disease, making things more exact, and lowering the possibility of any misdiagnoses. With real stories and studies, you've read how AI is changing health care for the better.

AI's power to enhance the healthcare experience, and not replace human interaction, is an essential element. It's another tool medical professionals can use that enables them to zero in on patient-centered care; implementing AI into their day-to-day routines. We've shown how when an organization is open to change, involves their staff in the process, and implements new technology, the experience can be beneficial for everyone involved.

Navigating the changing landscape of AI will require a lot of care. Keeping patient data confidential is the law, so ethics plays an essential role, meaning we must ensure the use of AI is transparent, and responsible. It's critical to be up-to-date, and invested, with the technological advances that are coming; integrating it into what already exists. It's also important to be smart about AI, whether you're involved in the technical aspect, work in healthcare, or are a policy maker.

Understanding what AI can realistically do, is a huge step towards integrating it into everyday medicine; being mindful of what its purpose will be in the future. Moving forward, AI will play an even larger part in the healthcare field; combining it with new technology like virtual reality, and genomics, making it much more personal. AI will also be able to identify health patterns, allowing us to preemptively diagnose any possible future illnesses. By using every resource available to us, we can completely change how we look after our patients.

As a final note, I'm asking you to do something meaningful. Please take the time to think about AI, and whether, or not, you believe it will be beneficial in your work. If these new technological advances can help you achieve your goals, don't ignore them! Your decision to utilize these tools can lead to significant changes in healthcare, and vastly improve the interactions you have with the people you care for. In a nut shell, your decision plays an essential role in the future of medicine!

Thank you for taking this journey into AI with me! Your enthusiasm for learning new things, and dedication to revamping healthcare for the better, inspires me. This book gives you crucial information, and suggestions, on how you can become an integral part of the fascinating world of AI. Always remember...when we embrace the possibilities of the future, we can actually create it. Let's do it together!

References

AI Chatbots in Healthcare | Benefits, Use Cases & Impact https://smartmedhx.ai/trends/ai-chatbots-in-healthcare/

Transforming healthcare with AI: The impact on ... https://www.mckinsey.com/industries/healthcare/our-insights/transforming-healthcare-with-ai

Ethical implications of AI and robotics in healthcare: A review https://pmc.ncbi.nlm.nih.gov/articles/PMC10727550/

Johns Hopkins inHealth Precision Medicine Initiative https://www.biostat.jhsph.edu/resource/inHealth_2024.pdf

Navigating the Path to AI Adoption in Healthcare: 5 Steps ... https://www.healthcareittoday.com/2024/01/09/navigating-the-path-to-ai-adoption-in-healthcare-5-steps-for-success/

How Innovations in Telemedicine, Wearables, and AI- ... https://blog.adrianalacyconsulting.com/telemedicine-wearables-ai-diagnostics-patient-care/

How AI-Powered Wearables are Reshaping Health Care https://www.captechu.edu/blog/how-ai-powered-wearables-are-reshaping-health-care

Overcoming key challenges in AI for healthcare https://www.zuehlke.com/en/insights/the-four-challenges-blocking-ai-in-healthcare-and-how-to-solve-them

4 ways AI is transforming healthcare | World Economic Forum https://www.weforum.org/stories/2024/11/ai-transforming-global-health/

AI in Healthcare - eCornell - Cornell University https://ecornell.cornell.edu/certificates/healthcare/ai-in-healthcare/

Collaborative Intelligence: How AI and Physicians Can ... https://www.smartbloodanalytics.com/en/waiting-room/collaborative-intelligence-how-ai-and-physicians-can-work-together-for-better-healthcare-outcomes-2354956

Preparing healthcare talent for an AI-powered future https://www.guild.com/latest-insights/preparing-healthcare-talent-for-an-ai-powered-future

WHO calls for safe and ethical AI for health https://www.who.int/news/item/16-05-2023-who-calls-for-safe-and-ethical-ai-for-health

The Intersection of GDPR and AI and 6 Compliance Best ... https://www.exabeam.com/explainers/gdpr-compliance/the-intersection-of-gdpr-and-ai-and-6-compliance-best-practices/

Algorithmic Bias in Health Care Exacerbates Social Inequities https://www.hsph.harvard.edu/ecpe/how-to-prevent-algorithmic-bias-in-health-care/

Federal Government Addresses AI Transparency and ... https://www.bakerlaw.com/insights/federal-government-addresses-ai-transparency-and-safety-in-healthcare/

10 AI in Healthcare Case Studies [2024] https://digitaldefynd.com/IQ/ai-in-healthcare-case-studies/

110   References

Advancements in Robotic Surgery: A Comprehensive ... https://pmc.ncbi.nlm.nih.gov/arti
cles/PMC10784205/

Virtual Health Assistants: Supporting Chronic Condition Care https://calciumhealth.com/
virtual-health-assistants-supporting-chronic-condition-care/page/3/?et_blog

Implementation of prediction models in the emergency ... https://pmc.ncbi.nlm.nih.gov/arti
cles/PMC9097992/

AI Investments Dominate Healthcare https://www.svb.com/news/company-news/ai-
investments-dominate-healthcare--silicon-valley-bank-releases-new-ai-patient-
journey-report/

Top AI Healthcare Startups to Watch in 2023 https://www.jorie.ai/post/top-ai-healthcare-
startups-to-watch-in-2023

The Ethics of AI in Healthcare https://hitrustalliance.net/blog/the-ethics-of-ai-in-health
care

Top 10 Startups Leading in Drug Discovery using AI https://www.greyb.com/blog/ai-drug-
discovery-startups/

FDA strengthens AI regulation to ensure patient safety and ... https://www.news-medical.
net/news/20241016/FDA-strengthens-AI-regulation-to-ensure-patient-safety-
and-innovation-in-healthcare.aspx

European Medicines Agency publishes five-year AI workplan https://www.dlapiper.com/en/
insights/publications/2024/01/european-medicines-agency-publishes-five-year-ai-
workplan

Key Elements of an AI Governance Program in Healthcare https://www.ailawandpolicy.
com/2024/08/key-elements-of-an-ai-governance-program-in-healthcare/

Integrating artificial intelligence into healthcare systems https://www.nature.com/articles/
s41746-024-01066-z

How Americans View Use of AI in Health Care ... https://www.pewresearch.org/science/
2023/02/22/60-of-americans-would-be-uncomfortable-with-provider-relying-on-
ai-in-their-own-health-care/

AI in Healthcare: Real-World Success Stories and Case ... https://www.linkedin.com/pulse/
ai-healthcare-real-world-success-stories-case-studies-avinash-chander-m9tic

AI-Supported Tool Can Help Reduce Misdiagnosis https://www.technologynetworks.com/
diagnostics/news/ai-supported-tool-can-help-reduce-misdiagnosis-380235

Human-AI Collaboration in Health Care https://www.scu.edu/ethics/healthcare-ethics-
blog/human-ai-collaboration-in-health-care/

Microsoft makes the promise of AI in healthcare real through ... https://blogs.microsoft.com/
blog/2024/03/11/microsoft-makes-the-promise-of-ai-in-healthcare-real-through-
new-collaborations-with-healthcare-organizations-and-partners/

Collaboration Best Practices for AI Teams | Restackio https://www.restack.io/p/collabora
tive-ai-systems-answer-collaboration-best-practices-cat-ai

Artificial intelligence in healthcare: transforming the practice of ... https://pmc.ncbi.nlm.nih.
gov/articles/PMC8285156/

The Impact of AI on the Healthcare Workforce https://www.himss.org/resources/impact-
ai-healthcare-workforce-balancing-opportunities-and-challenges

Generative AI in healthcare: Adoption trends and what's next https://www.mckinsey.com/

industries/healthcare/our-insights/generative-ai-in-healthcare-adoption-trends-and-whats-next

AI's role in revolutionizing personalized medicine by ... https://www.sciencedirect.com/science/article/pii/S2949866X2400087X

10 Case Studies of Successful Implementation of AI in ... https://scimedian.in/10-case-studies-of-successful-implementation-of-ai-in-healthcare/

The Ethics of AI in Healthcare https://hitrustalliance.net/blog/the-ethics-of-ai-in-healthcare

Artificial Intelligence in Global Health: Defining a Collective ... https://www.usaid.gov/cii/ai-in-global-health

Leveraging AI Tools to Bridge the Healthcare Gap in Rural Areas https://www.medrxiv.org/content/10.1101/2024.07.30.24311228v1.full-text

Global Initiative on AI for Health https://www.who.int/initiatives/global-initiative-on-ai-for-health

AI-Driven Healthcare Solutions Worldwide | International Journal of ... https://internationaljournals.org/index.php/ijtd/article/view/25?articlesBySameAuthorPage=4

Help Keep the Conversation Going!

Now that you've explored the exciting world of *AI In Healthcare*, it's your turn to share what you've learned, and inspire others to join in the journey.

By leaving your honest review on Amazon, you'll help other curious readers discover how this book can guide them through the fascinating intersection of technology, and medicine. Your thoughts could be what they need to take their first steps into understanding AI in healthcare.

Why Your Review Matters

Every review helps keep the conversation alive. By sharing your experience, you're contributing to the growth of knowledge, and ensuring that the exciting possibilities of AI in healthcare continue to reach more people.

I appreciate your support. Together, we can pass on this understanding, and keep the future of healthcare innovation alive.

Your opinion matters: we can't wait to hear what you think!

Printed in Great Britain
by Amazon

59357376R00066